'I would say 80 per cent of my
involves reminding Christians
God's children. Why? Read thi
Krish Kandiah brilliantly weave .... his own
experience of adopting with biblical insight to show
how our adoption as God's children changes
everything.'
**Tim Chester, Pastor of Grace Church
Boroughbridge, faculty member of Crosslands
and author of *Enjoying God***

'This is Krish as we've come to expect him;
inspiring, wise and challenging. But it's also Krish
with his guard down, heart out, pain shared, with a
backstage pass to the wounds and the wonder
surrounding adoption. Krish helps us see what he's
been discovering – that God wants us, loves us,
adopts us and draws us into his heart and home, for
good. Grasping this secret will change everything.
Reading this book will too!'
**Rachel Gardner, President of Girls' Brigade and
author of *The Girl De-Construction Project***

'Not just "an interesting biblical theme" but a life-
changing truth that takes us into the heart of the
gospel; beautifully explained and explored from
Krish's own experience.'
**Paul Harcourt, National Leader of New Wine,
England**

'Krish is someone who has inspired our Church to see the Father's heart of God as more than just an abstract doctrine. Reframing adoption as an invitation into an enfleshed reality; a lived form of discipleship in which the rejected discover a sense of home amongst the people of God.'
Mark Sayers, Senior Leader of Red Church Melbourne, Australia and author of *Strange Days* and *Reappearing Church*

'This book will make you radically rethink what discipleship looks like in light of the greatest privilege that God has given us – the ability to call him our adopted Father.'
Rachel and Tim Hughes, Lead Pastors of Gas Street Church, Birmingham

'In *The Greatest Secret*, Dr Krish Kandiah pulls back the curtain to reveal perhaps the most astounding theme of Scripture: our adoption by God as his daughters and sons. He shows that this is the highest honour humans can experience. This adoption satisfies the cry of the human heart for a family relationship that provides us with unalienable security, identity and hope. It elevates us to a place of dignity and favour that is unattainable through our own efforts. May this wonderful book inspire multitudes to love and good deeds.'

Dr Rice Broocks, Co-founder of Every Nation Churches and bestselling author of *God's Not Dead*

'In this deeply personal and moving book, Krish Kandiah takes us closer to God's own heart. Why do we speak so little of our adoption as God's children? It took the experience of adopting a child for Krish to grasp the true meaning of the Fatherhood of God. And in the pages of *The Greatest Secret* he shares with us this life-changing revelation.'

Rev Dr Michael P. Jensen, Rector of St Mark's Anglican Church in Darling Point, Australia and author of *My God, My God: Is it Possible to Believe Anymore?*

'I started reading Krish's book and was immediately engrossed – such is the gift of his storytelling. *The Greatest Secret* is as relatable as it is eye-opening; giving fresh insight into a way to view life, the world, God and our relationship with him, through a completely different lens. It is refreshing to read a Christian book that is powerful in its vulnerability, rawness, and ultimately, its hope.'

Chine McDonald, Head of Media at Christian Aid and Thought for the Day presenter

THE GREATEST SECRET

Why being adopted into God's family changes everything

KRISH KANDIAH

HODDER &
STOUGHTON

First published in Great Britain in 2019 by Hodder & Stoughton
An Hachette UK company

1

Copyright © Krish Kandiah, 2019

The right of Krish Kandiah to be identified as the
Author of the Work has been asserted by him in accordance
with the Copyright, Designs and Patents Act 1988.

Unless indicated otherwise, Scripture quotations are taken from the Holy
Bible, New International Version (Anglicised edition). Copyright © 1979,
1984, 2011 by Biblica Inc.® Used by permission. All rights reserved.

A CIP catalogue record for this title is available from the British Library

Trade Paperback ISBN 978 1 529 37498 8
eBook ISBN 978 1 529 37500 8

Typeset in Ehrhardt MT by
Palimpsest Book Production Ltd, Falkirk, Stirlingshire

Printed and bound in Great Britain by Clays Ltd, Elcograf S.p.A.

Hodder & Stoughton policy is to use papers that are natural, renewable
and recyclable products and made from wood grown in sustainable forests.
The logging and manufacturing processes are expected to conform
to the environmental regulations of the country of origin.

Hodder & Stoughton Ltd
Carmelite House
50 Victoria Embankment
London EC4Y 0DZ

www.hodderfaith.com

To my adopted daughter

Contents

Introduction: How I lost my love for God – and the unlikely way I found it again   1

1. **The secret that changes everything about everything**   13
    A claim hidden in plain sight – and a clue to the meaning of life, the universe and everything.

2. **The secret that changes everything about me**   31
    Who am I when everyone is looking – and who cares anyway?

3. **The secret that changes everything about church**   51
    Why water is thicker than blood – and chaos more welcome than order.

4. **The secret that changes everything about prayer**   69
Fixing broken attachments – and finding new connections.

5. **The secret that changes everything about mission**   87
The missionary myth – and where we go from here.

6. **The secret that changes everything about the Bible**   103
The greatest story never told – and how to be part of the happily ever after.

7. **The secret that changes everything about worship**   119
Doing right things wrong – and putting wrong things right.

8. **The secret that changes everything about justice**   131
When it's just not fair – and it's right under our nose.

9. **The secret that changes everything about suffering**   145
When we can't resolve the problems – and we can embrace the suffering.

10. The secret that changes everything about holiness   163
Conforming to the family likeness – and daring to be different.

Epilogue: A letter   177

Endnotes   185

Introduction

How I lost my love for God – and the unlikely way I found it again

There are some secrets I am going to share with you – things I have only ever told a close circle of intimate friends and family. I will change some names, times and details to protect the innocent – and the guilty – because this story is ultimately not about them, or even about me, but about all of us. I begin with myself not because I seek your sympathy or because my experience is unique or in any sense worse than anyone else's. Actually, it is quite the opposite. I think more of us struggle to love God than we might realise, or be willing to admit.

I was perhaps an unlikely candidate to lose love for God. First of all, I was an 'active' Christian; I had been a missionary, a youth worker and a pastor before working as a theologian and church planter. I had shelves full of Christian books (some of which I had even written) and many Christian friends on my contact list (I had even had the privilege of bringing one or two of them to faith). I was happily married with three beautiful children who, at four, five and six years old, were still full of wonder at the world, still full of respect for their father and still nearly always in bed by 7.30 p.m. On top of that, I had landed a dream job at a prestigious university, which came with a rather wonderful house in a highly desirable post-code.

Despite all of this, suddenly, over the course of a year, I became engulfed by a darkness I could not escape from. I had never experienced a mental health problem at any prior point in my life, but the blackness of those days was so deep that I found myself, on a number of occasions, considering whether ending my life would be a mercy to the rest of the family. I lost my appetite and struggled to get to sleep at night. I woke up many mornings with numb hands having clenched my fists so tightly in my sleep that I had cut off the circulation to my fingers.

Spiritually, emotionally, mentally and physically . . . I was a mess.

A number of things had crept up on me to contribute to this low point in my life. The main one was that the dream job I had landed – the one for which I had uprooted my young family – turned out to be, in fact, the stuff of nightmares. Perhaps I should have seen the warning signs earlier. When my boss started slamming the phone down on me. When my colleagues began lawyering up. When false allegations were made against other staff members. When I walked past a noticeboard and saw my own job being advertised. When I was press-ganged into signing disclaimers against taking legal action against my employer. By the time I realised how serious all this was, I felt acutely aware that if I lost my job, my family would be made – temporarily at least – homeless. But I also knew that if I stuck with the job, the toxic and hostile environment would damage me, my mental health and my family irrevocably. Perhaps you know something about feeling trapped, disempowered, disregarded, intimidated. It eats away at your spirit. It tortures your soul. It changes you.

This was not my first experience of being bullied. When I was a child, I was relentlessly hounded because of the colour of my skin. At that time I found that God's unshakeable love for me, the support of my church family and the encouragement of the Holy Spirit gave me the backbone I needed to walk tall no matter how much spit and spite erupted from the mouths of my fellow comprehensive schoolboys. Nor was it the first time I had been threatened with losing my job and my home. As a young married couple, my wife and I had once found ourselves working in a city where constant deafening machine-gun fire rattled our windows and caused us to sleep fully clothed on the floor under a table, a bag packed in case of the need for sudden evacuation. At that time the words of the Psalms gave me hope, and the Holy Spirit came close, giving me peace to trust God, my shield and refuge.

So what was different this time? There were no bullets flying. There were no fists raised to my face. I had friends. I had my wonderful, wondering children around me. In hindsight, I almost lost my mind and my faith because the root of the evil appeared to come from Christians. They were part of the religious establishment. They were well-known speakers who one moment could tell moving stories from the stage about the grace of God and the next, stab colleagues in the back with disparaging remarks, vicious threats and lawsuits. Some went to the same church as me and sang praise to God in the same room. We ate together the bread that symbolised the death of Christ for all of us, drinking from the same cup that represented Jesus' spilt blood. The next day at work they couldn't even look me in the eye. This behaviour of other Christians felt like it was robbing me of the resources to be able to cope. My faith and my family in faith had always been my rock. Now those foundations were being eroded, undermined by the actions of those who claimed to know – and, worse, teach – about God. My safe place, my source of strength had been compromised.

In the middle of that year my mother called me and asked me to go with her to an appointment with an oncologist. The news was not great. She had stage 4 ovarian cancer and there was very little they could do to treat it. I remember getting home, locking myself in the bathroom and sitting on the edge of the bath feeling upset that my mother had chosen such an inconvenient time to begin to die. I didn't know how I was going to cope, nor how I could be a good father and husband while this was going on. And then I remember being hit by my utter selfishness in being more concerned about how this was going to affect me than about how my mother would cope.

I had a degree in medicinal chemistry, but I couldn't stop the cancer. Instead, I clung to a small tin of aromatherapy balm that promised to help me sleep. I had a PhD in theology, but I couldn't find any sense in what God was trying to teach me. Instead, I stumbled across occasional solace in the bedtime Bible stories I read to my young children. I had years of experience of being a pastor, but all my tried and trusted methods of helping people persevere and hold on to faith in difficult circumstances now seemed pathetic. I found it very difficult even to think about God, let alone love him.

I was too weak to face up effectively to the bullying at work, and I was too weak to be able to trust God. I was too weak to support my family and I was too weak to help my mother. I felt a failure.

I meet many people in these sorts of rock-bottom

places. Bad things have happened to them, and the very people who could be helping them up out of the pit seem to be pushing them back down again. When we are in that position, there seems to be no hope. We begin to believe that God has abandoned us. Our faith weighs us down instead of buoying us up through the storms.

I am writing this book more than ten years after that dreadful time in my life. I couldn't see it at the time, but God had not abandoned me. It's just that he wasn't quite where I expected him to be, and he wasn't doing quite what I expected him to do. God is like that. He is higher, greater, more mysterious than we sometimes like to think. 'For I know the plans I have for you,' he says in Jeremiah 29:11. He knows the plans and we don't. He has plans to give us hope and a way forward, even when we are feeling hopeless and directionless.

God's plan for me was a most unlikely plan, seeded years, maybe generations, earlier. My wife and I had both grown up hearing first-hand stories of orphanages around the world. Both our mothers, for very different reasons, had found themselves living in homes for vulnerable children. And so it had seemed entirely natural for us when we got married and had children of our own to offer our home and family as a safe place for children in need to be loved and cared for. The process to become foster and adoptive parents got off to a terrible start when we failed the initial telephone screening. Our deficiency? Not enough bedrooms in our otherwise sizeable West London home. So that was the end of our fostering and adoption journey. Until, that is, a job came up at a prestigious university with a rather wonderful house thrown in for good measure. Suddenly we sailed through the thorough home assessment, background checks and intense panel interrogation and, before we knew it, we were caring for a beautiful newborn baby girl.

Over the next twelve months, as both my situation at work and my mum's health deteriorated, this little girl grew and thrived. When I couldn't sleep at night, her presence provided a little company. When I was drowning in my sadness, her infectious giggle was a lifeline of brightness. When I couldn't pray, I pushed a buggy round the block and spoon-fed pureed fruit into an appreciative, hungry, toothless mouth, and at least one of us was gently nourished and nurtured.

And then came 11 September. This was the date we went to court to adopt that little girl formally into our family. It is, of course, a date that brings to mind the worst atrocities humankind can wreak against itself. But for me that date will always signify one of the highlights of my life. Perhaps it shines even brighter because of the darkness that surrounded it, the darkness of terrorism wherever and whenever it occurs. The darkness of a world full of cancer, and mental health crises, and children removed by law from parents who had not been protected themselves when they were young. The darkness of a world where workplace bullying is allowed to continue unchecked.

I never did rediscover my previous relationship with God. I say that because I encountered a whole new relationship with him. My family had grown from five to six and then to seven as we fostered another little boy. We had moved house and job and community again, not knowing what the future would hold. There were a lot of strange connections and new relationships unfolding. I always knew that God was my father, and that I was his child, but after 11 September my developing relationship with my adopted daughter opened my eyes to the truth that God was my *adoptive* father, and I was his *adopted* child.

That changed everything.

Imagine you were to attend a family get-together today – perhaps a birthday party or an anniversary. The sort of event where your distant relatives appear – the relations you usually forget you have. The sort of event with lots of food and little expectation, and children running around the crowded rooms. These are the events that end with the leftovers being boxed up for guests to take home and people saying they ought to do this more often. Imagine, at this get-together, that an elderly aunt drinks a little too much champagne and, while she's telling all the old familiar stories, she lets slip a family secret and utters the party-stopping words: 'Didn't you know, dear? You're adopted!'

This has actually happened to friends of mine. When they try to explain what it feels like to hear those words, they liken it to experiencing an earthquake, as though the firm ground beneath their feet had given way. You lose your balance and are sent into mental and emotional freefall. In a heartbeat, those you thought were your family feel like strangers, and strangers are somehow family. The cracks come to the surface and you begin to see or imagine the cover-ups, the conspiracies, the lies. You wonder who you are, where you have come from, and what you are going to do with yourself now. Adoption changes everything.

My daughter will never have that earthquake moment because she has always known she was adopted. That does not mean she will not struggle with seismic issues of identity and belonging, but it does mean she is piecing together her life story with the knowledge that she was once loved and lost, but also loved and found. She was chosen and welcomed unconditionally despite the mysteries of turmoil in her biological ancestry, and regardless of what the future may hold. She both blends in and stands out in her adoptive family. Whether she is learning to sing, or giving blood, or sitting exams, or brushing her hair, she is growing up with an awareness that adoption and its aftershocks somehow impact everything.

When we adopted her, I felt something of the ground-shattering force of suddenly realising my own identity as an adopted child of God and how this affects every aspect of my life and faith. Over time this realisation has substantially shifted the way I view myself, and the way I view people around me. It has made me question what I really know of God. It has exposed some of the cover-ups, conspiracies and lies regarding my faith to which I had previously been blind. It has also revealed some of the untold treasures and mysteries of the gospel that I may otherwise never have discovered.

I wrote this book for two reasons. First, because I meet many people who have similar secrets to me. People who struggle to find God and to love him. Perhaps this struggle is because of difficulties at work or with health or church. Perhaps it is because of the terrible things we see on the news or hear about in our own communities. Perhaps it is because we sense that there is some sort of cover-up going on when it comes to faith. Perhaps it is for totally different reasons. From my experience and from talking to others it seems that many more of us struggle to grasp God's love than we might expect. There are swathes of us who find ourselves feeling that we don't quite fit in, wondering if we have lost out when it comes to faith, to life. I wonder if God wants you to know that you are his adopted child? Exploring some of the implications of this truth could change everything.

I also wrote this book for my daughter and for those like her, forging a way through complex family dynamics, wondering how faith fits into all that. As she approaches her teenage years, I know that for many adopted children this time can be particularly challenging as they grapple with huge questions about their identity and their parentage and with how to make sense of the story of their lives. Whatever happens, I want her to know that she is mine. I will not give up on her. I will not be going anywhere. I love her fiercely. I wonder if God wants you to know a Father like this – perfectly like this? Many of us experience the anxiety of not being sure if we are really good enough, or if we really belong somewhere, or if we are truly loved, or if we can really trust anyone. Many of us struggle to make sense of our life stories – we have unexplained or unresolved episodes in our lives that we long to piece together. Understanding that God is our adoptive Father could begin to change everything.

Adoption has been a dirty secret in the Church for too long. There have, indeed, been cover-ups perpetuated to avoid talking about it. Our pastors and youth leaders have much preferred to preach and talk about forgiveness or rescue, about freedom and redemption, without noticing that without the missing ingredient of adoption even these amazing truths are impoverished. The theme of adoption is neglected in our pulpits, our songs, our programmes and our gospel, even though it is present throughout our Bibles, from Job to Jesus, from Moses to Paul, from the prophets to the epistles. Failing to reflect on or to celebrate our adoption skews our faith, limits our relationship with God and undermines our sense of identity, purpose and confidence. The good news is that everything can change. Instead of a flawed sub-biblical understanding of Christianity, the Spirit of adoption wants to seismically recast the way we understand faith, read Scripture, practise discipleship and experience God's love.

It wasn't my PhD in theology that helped me unlock new depths to my relationship with the God who adopted me, nor was it my role in the divinity faculty at a prestigious university. It was a baby girl who appeared in my life at just the right time. Sometimes, I think she saved my life. I wonder if she can save yours too?

Chapter 1

The secret that changes everything about everything

A claim hidden in plain sight – and a clue to the meaning of life, the universe and everything.

In an uncharacteristic, quavering voice she whispered, 'May I have a word?' The hairdresser had just finished and Jazbinda was adeptly applying her make-up while everyone kept telling her she looked radiant in her wedding dress. But her mother couldn't keep eye contact while she murmured: 'I thought you should know, you know, before . . .' As she walked down the aisle, Jazbinda's legs felt like they would buckle beneath her. When the priest asked her if she, 'Jazbinda Shah', would take Brian Jones to be her husband, she didn't know how to answer, because she didn't know who she was any more. As she paused, everyone in the chapel held their breath.

Bill had been tasked with clearing out the attic. His mother's house needed to be emptied quickly so it could be sold to pay for her care. It was so hard watching her health deteriorate, watching strangers nurse the one who had nursed him, watching the family home slowly declutter and de-personalise. As he moved one box after another, he noticed a half-open envelope with a picture inside he had never seen before. It was him as a toddler, in the arms of a woman of whom he had no recollection. On the back of the photo was his birthdate, but next to a different name. That was the day his world changed.

A dirty secret

Adoption has, for many generations, been a dirty secret, something of which to be ashamed, to be sealed in an envelope, to be boxed in the attic with the dust. It is a word best whispered, if spoken at all. Adoption became, at some point in history, synonymous with failure. Didn't it seem to shout infertility or impotence or illicit relations? Didn't it declare to the world that the adults involved were somehow defective, without the physical capacity to produce offspring and forced to accept someone else's cast-off children? While other people could get pregnant by accident and far too often, it seemed, why, despite their most determined efforts, couldn't certain couples get things to happen and why was it them who had to resort to plan B, the booby-prize option of adoption? Didn't an adoption journey go hand in hand with pain, disappointment, shame and feelings of inadequacy and failure? Didn't it undermine a sense of identity, a sense of masculinity or femininity? Didn't it underline an incompetency to parent? The shadow fell across the children, too. Were they deficient, unwanted kids of birth parents, and plan-B kids of adoptive parents? Talking about adoption only brought these heartaches and questions to the surface, and so it was best to hide it, bury it, silence it. Adoption became the dirty secret that was only revealed by accident or in an emergency.

Adoption, the act of legally taking in a child to raise as your own, never needs to incur or imply such feelings of shame and failure. In fact, films present it in a whole different angle. According to Hollywood, children who come from foster homes can be superheroes saving the world from evil beings such as Voldemort, Darth Vader, Lord Sauron or Dr No. Those adopting such children can be well-respected heroes like Jean Valjean in *Les Misérables* as well as well-meaning villains like *Despicable Me*'s Felonius Gru, or Batman.[1]

But while adoption has been celebrated in fiction and science fiction, it has too often continued to be a dirty secret in real life. Somehow this negative misperception of adoption seems to have infected the Christian faith too, causing generations to have neglected the Bible's teaching on the subject. It has become what some might call a Cinderella subject.

Just like the unwanted stepdaughter in the fairy tale, the doctrine of adoption was deemed to be an embarrassment, locked away from the public eye, not given the attention or honour it deserved, and definitely not permitted to come to the ball. It didn't get invited to the worship parties or the conference main stage. Instead it was banished to the cellar. Perhaps it would be let out when all the endless chores were done.

We know how the story ends. The silenced and forgotten one, downtrodden, unacknowledged and unappreciated, turns out to be more precious and beautiful than anyone could have imagined. Once she is discovered and given her rightful place, due honour is bestowed on her. The whole kingdom celebrates.

A Cinderella revolution

It's time for a Cinderella revolution. The one who is neglected needs to be celebrated. The one who is forgotten needs to be remembered. The one who is suppressed needs to be liberated. It's time for a seismic reversal. We need to pull the doctrine of adoption out of the dust and ashes and display it with all the glory it deserves. And guess what? The shoe fits. We don't have to cut our gospel down or squeeze it awkwardly out of shape to accommodate this strange new doctrine. Quite the opposite – it fits together perfectly with our faith because it was always meant to. Everything we value most about life, faith and the universe makes better sense when we understand God's adoption of us. It does not have to be a dirty secret. It is the key to unlocking untold riches, joys and treasures of the Christian faith.

Perhaps you think that sounds slightly ambitious, dramatic, overblown. Maybe it reminds you of one of the many books that over-promise and under-deliver – the get-rich-quick book, the transform-your-prayer-life book, the everything-you-need-to-know-about-decision-making book, the ultimate-diet bible. I should know as I have read most of them (although I decided not to read the decision-making one). They offer so much, but ultimately fail to deliver. I never want to write a book like that. But here I am saying that understanding our adoption may just be the secret to everything – our true identity, our prayer life, our church life, our family life, our hopes and dreams, our history and our future, the meaning of the universe. I can only make such fantastic claims because this secret has been fully accessible for two millennia. It is written in clear and unmistakable language in the world's best-selling book, in one of its most influential sections in one of its most beloved chapters: Romans, chapter 8.

A momentous revelation

This is the apostle Paul writing. The persecu-
tor-turned-preacher. The man who was on a
search-and-destroy mission against the Church, yet
who miraculously became its chief architect and
agitant. This is the letter to the Roman Church, arguably Paul's finest God-inspired work, that
singlehandedly is credited as igniting the Reformation
that transformed not just the Church, but the entirety
of western culture itself. This is Romans 8, the chapter
that millions of Christians around the world treasure
because of its soaring prose and stellar promises. This
is the chapter that begins with the liberating truth
that there is 'now no condemnation for those who are
in Christ Jesus',[2] and ends with the stirring conviction
that nothing, not anything, can 'separate us from the
love of God'.[3] This is the same chapter containing the
beautiful promise that assures us that 'in all things
God works for the good of those who love him'.[4]

But for all the affection there is for Paul's theological masterpiece, for all the recognition of the
emphasis on God's grace, and God's sovereignty, and
God's love, too many of us have missed the proverbial
wood for the trees. I certainly did, despite years of
teaching this passage to congregations, to young
people and to students. For at the heart of this passage
is a momentous revelation:

We know that the whole creation has been groaning as in the pains of childbirth right up to the present time. Not only so, but we ourselves, who have the firstfruits of the Spirit, groan inwardly as we wait eagerly for our adoption, the redemption of our bodies. For in this hope we were saved.

(Romans 8:22–4)

This passage is immense. It references the creation, touches on the fall of humanity with the resulting pains of childbirth and the frustrations the world now experiences, then homes in on our salvation and the incomparable gift of the Holy Spirit, and ends up with the restoration of all things – a new heaven and earth. This is a cosmic canvas on which the secret to the universe is revealed. Our creation, our destination, our salvation – or, in other words, life, death and the universe – are all awaiting, building up to, straining towards . . . our adoption!

If our adoption truly is the event that all of creation has been waiting for, it should change everything. This truth gives us a new lens through which to understand the whole of our lives and the entirety of our Christian experience. It offers us a new perspective on every facet of our discipleship. The metaphor of adoption can radically alter the way we read and understand the Bible. Our adopted status should impact the way we relate to others around us. The sacrament of adoption transforms how we approach our relationship with our Father God. The doctrine of adoption reframes our understanding of our own salvation. The experience of adoption could even affect who is welcomed into our own families.

Adoption is arguably the Christian faith's greatest secret. Great in its place in God's plan for the universe. Great in its capacity to reform our life and faith. Great in its brilliance and promise and purpose. But also greatly undervalued, greatly underappreciated and greatly underemphasised.

Perhaps one of the reasons we have been missing the vastness of the revelation that adoption is the key to everything is because of Paul's downright honesty. Although the chapter is full of echoes of the origin story of the universe, and full of references to our eternal hope, Paul does not underplay the frustrations of real life in the here and now. From sin to suffering to separation anxiety, from our struggles with prayer to our struggles with relating to God, Paul is not afraid to call it out. Maybe you recognise in yourself a sense of dissatisfaction with even the best things in life, a continual disappointment that things don't deliver what you hope for, the sense that you don't really belong. If you recognise some of these frustrations then you are in good company because, according to the letter to the Romans, frustration, whether we like it or not, is the new normal. The frustration we feel is part of that bigger plan, the secret story woven into the very fabric of the universe itself, a narrative arc that is slowly but steadily working itself out from the very beginning to the very end, a journey towards our adoption.

Paul has found a way to have his feet on the ground and his head in the air. He holds on to the hope of the gospel amid the turmoil of everyday life. How can he do this? He sees that the two are intrinsically linked: the frustrations we experience have a purpose. God has deliberately allowed the captivity of the cosmos – in order eventually to set it free. The universe is not reeling out of control, it is not a gigantic accident or some kind of cosmic juggernaut careering unstoppably towards celestial havoc. We are told that even in the trouble and the tragedy God is doing something. While there is cancer and childlessness, while there are mental health problems and injustice, poverty, betrayal and death, there is also hope. While there is great frustration, there is also great expectation.

When faced with the catalogue of struggles that we experience in the world, it is very easy to fall into thought patterns of fear or hopelessness. If anyone understood this, it was Paul – he was only too familiar with suffering, persecution, betrayal and ongoing excruciating pain. He had seen others die, and he fully expected himself to be killed for his message. But he had a secret weapon against fear and hopelessness. Except it was not so secret – again he gives it away in

Romans 8, showing that he understands not only the purpose of adoption but also the power of adoption.

Paul writes that it is the power of the Spirit of adoption – the one that enables us to trust in our Abba Father – that can help us overcome fear:

> *The Spirit you received does not make you slaves, so that you live in fear again; rather, the Spirit you received brought about your adoption to sonship. And by him we cry, 'Abba, Father.' The Spirit himself testifies with our spirit that we are God's children. Now if we are children, then we are heirs – heirs of God and co-heirs with Christ, if indeed we share in his sufferings in order that we may also share in his glory.*
>
> *(Romans 8:15–17)*

Paul writes that it is the power of the Spirit of adoption – the one who lives in us, representing the first fruits of what is to come, a taster of God's overall plan – that can help us overcome hopelessness:

> *We ourselves, who have the firstfruits of the Spirit, groan inwardly as we wait eagerly for our adoption to sonship, the redemption of our bodies. For in this hope we were saved. But hope that is seen is no hope at all. Who hopes for what they already have? But if we hope for what we do not yet have, we wait for it patiently.*
>
> *(Romans 8:23–5)*

In other words, not only does adoption help us understand the problems of the world, it also helps us handle them. The doctrine of adoption gives us purpose *and* power, perspective *and* peace. It enables us to see the big picture of what life is really all about, and it empowers us to deal with life on a day-to-day basis.

That really should change everything about everything.

A now and a not yet

There is a fundamental reason adoption can be both pragmatic and paramount, both empowering and inspiring, both a premise and a promise, and that is because it is both now and not yet. The paradox is there in Romans 8. In verse 15 it appears our adoption has already happened – we receive the Spirit of sonship when we become Christians and now we can call God our *Abba* Father. However, in verse 23 it seems as though we are waiting for our adoption in the future at the end of time. How can both of these be true at the same time?

My daughter was legally adopted when she was two years old, and after she had lived with us for most of her life to that point. But that was not the end of the story, it was just the beginning. Imagine if I had walked out of the courtroom and left her on the steps of the building, saying that all the fight and work I had put into securing her as my daughter was now complete. You would think that was mad. The whole point of adoption is not about the change of status, it is about the change of relationship. Pursuing the legalities was not the consummation of our efforts, it was the conception of an intimate, committed relationship that is still being worked out and developed today. It is true that had I walked out of the courtroom and straight under a bus, she would have been just as eligible to inherit her share of my estate as if I were to live to be 100 years old. But although she was always 100 per cent adopted, there was – and there still is – so much more about our relationship to discover and develop.

This is how we reconcile the fact that we have both been adopted and long for the fulfilment of it. We have a taste of it, but there is so much more to discover. We may sense some sort of intimacy with God, but it is just the beginning, and it leaves us desperately wanting more. It is a frustrating tension. I know many Christians who throw in the towel because their relationship with God does not feel as significant, real or immediate as they sense it should. When their expectations of intimacy with God are not met they walk away from it. But it can also be a joyful tension. Like our anticipation before a holiday, which builds with the emptying of the fridge and the filling of the suitcases, we can cope with the temporary chaos because there are treasures untold yet to come that will be worth the wait.

An act of grace

But before we begin to look at those tensions and treasures of our faith more closely, we must first ask, *Why?* Why is adoption the destination to which all of human history is heading? Why is the fulfilment of our adoption the moment for which creation holds its breath? Why does it empower us to face hardships? Why is the promise of adoption worth waiting for, worth the frustrations and struggles of day-to-day life?

For many people, adoption is merely considered the third and worst way to have a child. There's natural birth. If that doesn't work, for some there is in vitro fertilisation (IVF), and if that doesn't work, well, there's always adoption. But that is not God's approach to adoption. God was not incapable of having his own children, he was not bored or lonely. God did not adopt us because *he* needed it. God adopted us because *we* needed it. God saw that we were enslaved and vulnerable and he stepped up and became what we need him to be, a Father who would go to the ends of the earth for us, who would die for us, who would give us the world, who would put everything right. God adopted us as a wonderful act of mercy, compassion and altruistic grace.

I began to realise how much I had misunderstood

the doctrine of adoption when we legally adopted our little girl. Our three birth children were all we could ever have wanted or dreamed for. We did not set out on our fostering journey to adopt a fourth child. But when a social worker sat in my front room and said that the baby in my arms could not return to her birth family and might never recover from a move to yet another new family on top of everything else she had been through, I knew I had no choice. This child needed adopting, and she needed adopting by my family, whatever sacrifices and changes that would entail. If God was willing to go to such extraordinary lengths to include me in his family, even allowing his son Jesus to lay down his life for me, then I had to mirror that in this decision. Little did I know then that in seeking to emulate what little I understood of God's love, I would rediscover God's love in a whole new way.

The family we know as God – Father, Son and Holy Spirit – longs to welcome us into the intimacy of God's love. God has gone to incredible lengths to ensure that the way is cleared for us to come home with him. In his letter to the Galatian Church, Paul ties adoption to the heart of the gospel itself:

> *But when the set time had fully come, God sent his Son, born of a woman, born under the law, to redeem those under the law, that we might receive adoption to sonship.*
> *(Galatians 4:4–5)*

God, the Holy Trinity, knows the history, the problems, the potentials for disaster in adopting us, but they want us in their forever family anyway. The journey to adopt us began long before we were born, long before the world was created. As Paul writes again, this time in his letter to the Church in Ephesus:

> *For he chose us in him before the creation of the world to be holy and blameless in his sight. In love he predestined us for adoption to sonship through Jesus Christ, in accordance with his pleasure and will – to the praise of his glorious grace, which he has freely given us in the One he loves.*
>
> *(Ephesians 1:4–6)*

And why? Because adoption demonstrates the compassion of God as he welcomes lost and vulnerable children into his family. Because adoption manifests the faithfulness of God that has been and will be committed to us for eternity. Because adoption displays the love of God as he is willing to embrace us as his children for ever. Because adoption highlights the grace of God as there is nothing we have done or will do to deserve it or earn it.

We need to get rid of the shame around adoption and see it in all its glory. This may have been easier for Paul because in Roman times adoption was already seen as a high privilege. It was often connected with inheritance, as families deliberately chose heirs they could trust with running their businesses or their families, or even their nations. In the Roman Empire, even Emperor Nero and his four predecessors were all adopted, and in turn adopted sons who would succeed them.[5]

Roman adoption was such an honour that it could be a huge insult to existing members of a family, as it implied that the birth sons of the emperor or the business owner or the head of the family were seen as not being up to the task, as being incapable or not credible enough to take on the role. Paul radicalises and reboots the Roman understanding of adoption because there is no question that Jesus is the best son the universe has seen. God the Father has full confidence in his perfect son Jesus Christ, and yet he still grants us the privilege of being adopted as his sons and daughters. Paul also radicalises and reboots a modern-day understanding of adoption: being part of God's family is indeed a privilege – freely and lovingly bestowed on us, no matter where we've come from, and regardless of what we've done or how unworthy we feel.

Adoption is the secret that changes everything about everything. Once we begin to see it, it is hard to avoid. I wonder what difference it would make if our adoption into God's family became not only more openly discussed and more widely celebrated, but, as in Paul's train of thought, the greatest generative metaphor for understanding the Christian faith and life.

In this book, as we work through the rich theme of adoption portrayed through Scripture, we will see how our lives can be caught up in the divine dynamic storyline that revolves around God bringing his lost children home, safe and sound. The revolution has begun. The dirty secret is no longer dirty, and is no longer a secret. The shame can be shaken off. The glory can be revealed. It is time to marvel as the truth begins to cascade the transforming grace of God throughout our hearts and minds. Nothing will be the same again.

~

Questions for reflection

1. What is your initial reaction to the idea of adoption? Where have these positive and negative views and preconceptions come from?

2. What surprises you most about Paul linking God's adoption of us to the meaning of the universe itself? Why do you think the doctrine of adoption is mentioned so little in our churches?

3. 'The shame can indeed be shaken off, and the glory revealed.' Where is the greatest potential for change in your life? How could a deeper understanding of adoption impact that?

Chapter 2

The secret that changes everything about me

Who am I when everyone is looking –
and who cares anyway?

As my aircraft broke through the cloud barrier I wanted to take a picture, but I was having plane shame. There was no way to capture this moment without including the logo of the budget airline I was flying with, and that would mess up the social media post. It's shallow and ridiculous, I know, but it continued to bug me during those beautiful aerial sunset moments.

Maybe that was why I was sympathetic as I read in the inflight newspaper the story of Anna Sorokin, who arrived in New York City presenting herself as a German heiress with $60m in assets and trying to get a loan of $22m for her foundation. She lived the high life, hiring private jets, attending the most elite parties and handing out $100 tips to bag carriers and Uber drivers. But Anna Sorokin, or rather Anna Delvey, was eventually caught out and found guilty of multiple counts of theft and grand larceny. It had all been a lie, a façade, a false identity.

Sorokin's audacity was shocking, and the reporter seemed to revel in delight that she got her comeuppance. But I felt equally condemned as I saw more of myself in Sorokin's manipulating behaviour than I wanted to admit. It reminded me of the guilt I felt when I read Clive Hamilton's insightful verdict on the challenge of our age in his book *Growth Fetish*: 'People buy things they don't need, with money they don't have, to impress people they don't like.'[1]

I know that my Twitter feed only presents the curated highlights of my life in a vain attempt to impress. The sun-soaked beach photo from a recent Miami trip was shared on my Instagram account rather than a picture of the dreary boardroom where I had spent most of my time. I posted a picture of the ornate dessert from a lunch with a client rather than one of the cheese on toast I made for the kids later that day. It is not just on social media that this manicured projected-self emerges. Sometimes when I check myself in the mirror before a significant meeting I realise that my expensive-looking outfit has been cobbled together from visits to the charity shop. Or as I look at the list of jobs and skills on my CV I know that, behind these headline highlights, there are many struggles and difficulties I choose not to disclose. I work hard to present the best possible version of myself to the world. But who am I really, and who am I trying to impress?

Whether it's me or Anna Sorokin, the desire to present a better version of ourselves than is really the case betrays an internal struggle to come to terms with who we are, or with who we would like to be, or with who we feel we should be. Dissatisfaction with our identity is a challenge for all of us. And things have become more complicated of late. What we might call 'personal identity' has been called into question in ways that our ancestors would never have dreamed possible. There are more things we can now choose about who we are and who we become than ever before. In days gone by, our status, our jobs, our social standing, our marital partners were all predetermined. If you were born a baker you would die a baker; if you were born a serf you would die a serf. But now a supermarket shelf stacker can become a rock star, a market trader can become a business tycoon. Not only that, we are immersed in advertising that tells us that buying the right aftershave, clothes or car can make us the kind of person we dream of becoming. Our identities can be carefully curated and constructed, and yet many of us are plagued with such self-doubt, such self-reproach and such low self-esteem that we struggle to understand who we truly are.[2]

This paradox hits me every time I travel to the house in which I was brought up. I was born in Brighton in the 1970s, and my father still lives in the family home. When I visit him, everything is pretty much the same as it was back then. It has the same geometrically tessellating brown and orange carpet in the hallways. The same avocado bathroom suite. The same yellow paisley sheets and pink chenille bedspreads on the same beds. The same dusty copies of *Reader's Digest* on the same shelves. It also has the same pictures hanging on the walls. They are pictures of a boy in desperate need of a haircut, sporting thick-rimmed glasses with his various school uniforms, or wearing one of the many brown corduroy outfits handed down to him by older cousins, and that knitted tank top his mother claimed he even wore to bed.

Who was that child? And what happened to him? In one sense they are photographs of me, but the 'me' I see myself as now is so very far removed from the 'me' that was that boy. And the 'me' others see or project is totally different again. Ask other people who I am and they may define me in terms of my job or my qualifications, my ethnicity or my faith, or in relation to the books or social media posts I have written. Local friends define me as 'the one with all the kids', or use some less polite way of describing an unusually large family. My children introduce me to their friends with a health warning that I will probably talk too much, ask too many questions, and tell terrible jokes. Who am I really?

The challenge with personal identity is that although it is absolutely fundamental, it is frustratingly difficult to pin down. This dichotomy has led to new levels of fluidity when it comes, for example, to our professional life, our styling and image, and even our sexual and gender identity. The long-term mental health implications of continually renegotiating who we are or how we present ourselves remain to be seen. Moreover, many of us are juggling multiple identities. Who we are in public and in private, at work and at home, in school and on social media is not always the same person.

The Church has had an answer to this for a long time. Our primary identity is our divinely given one – the person God made us to be. When we know that we are God's children, created, loved and chosen by him, belonging to him, shaped and protected by him, everything else becomes subsidiary. Sometimes the Church has been guilty of broadcasting this too loudly, and ignoring or over-simplifying the complexities of the issues involved. The Bible, from the first book to the last, recognises the challenges of our identity and factors that contribute to it. From the fracture lines to our sense of self recognised in the curse in Genesis, to the preservation of culture and language when the new heavens and the new earth are described in

Revelation,[3] Scripture gives us a nuanced and balanced framework to understand the very many factors differentiating one human being from another: race, ethnicity, age, gender, gifting, relationship status, health and vocation, to name but a few. Scripture also gives us clarity on the imperative of showing equal value, honour, dignity, love and respect to all people, whatever our difficulties and differences.[4] And it challenges us to respect the good gifts God gives us in the form of social structures such as government, Church and family that can help different people find the same security.

While nature and nurture, history and heritage may shape our identity – for better or worse – and must be taken into consideration, there is something fundamentally important about grasping the oft-neglected but nevertheless core teaching of the Church that has sustained millions of Christians for two millennia: we are God's children. Perhaps the Church has also been guilty of being too quiet about this. We are told clearly in Scripture that our identity in Christ as the children of God relativises every demographic difference, every social barrier, every class structure, every ethnic, gender and class division that separates and divides our societies:

So in Christ Jesus you are all children of God through faith, for all of you who were baptised into Christ have clothed yourself with Christ. There is neither Jew nor Gentile, neither slave nor free, nor is there male and female, for you are all one in Christ Jesus.

(Galatians 3:26–8)

I meet many Christians who struggle with their identity as God's children, and it is a struggle for which I have great sympathy. Just as I would rather not show you the pictures of me aged six in my father's house, so I would rather not, to be honest, talk about myself as a child of God. I'd rather show you pictures of me speaking to a packed room, or parade the most impressive version of my CV, or tell you about the important people who follow me on social media. When it comes to understanding my spiritual identity, I'd much rather see myself as an ambassador for Christ, an evangelist, a conqueror, an heir; these descriptors seem far more appealing, more heroic, more glorious. Defining myself as God's child can feel infantalising, disempowering, degrading even.

The struggles that come with identifying as a child of God may lead us to the conclusion that embracing our identity as an *adopted* child of God would be even harder. But what if the reverse was true? What if the truth of our spiritual adoption could in fact help us with all the various forms of our identity crises? What if adoption were the secret that changed everything about 'me'?

A day in court

As I stood before the judge with my polished boots squeaking and my heart racing, I felt out of place. I had tried to present myself as a worthy candidate for becoming an adopter and as a good father while the social workers had thoroughly scrutinised every aspect of my family's life. And now, here I was in my best suit trying to convince a judge that I was a well-meaning citizen who intended to give this little girl everything she could ever want or need.

The child wriggling in my arms was oblivious to any façade. She wasn't going to sit still or be quiet however much we had dressed her up for the occasion. She was oblivious to the anxieties racing through my mind: what happens if we fail? What if we are not deemed good enough? What if the judge rejects us as adopters because we are Christians? What if he finds me guilty of being a substandard father or a spiritual fraudster? She was oblivious to the location: a building where people go to be examined, cross-examined, judged, sentenced, punished. She was oblivious to the implications: that a man with a funny wig and a little hammer had the power to redesign her future, reassign her name, and realign her identity. That she would be stuck with us for the rest of her childhood. She was oblivious to the tears of relief and joy and excitement as we were finally declared a family. All she really was interested in was whether it was yet time to go to the ice-cream parlour adjacent to the courthouse, as promised.

I was not oblivious. I was only too aware of the agonising wait for the decision, of the fears and concerns that were making my heart race, of the significance of what was happening and the weight of the legal system, of the implications – that these four children beside me would be equally entitled to everything I could give them. I needn't have worried so much. The judge loved adoptions. He said it was the best part of his job and invited all of my children to come and sit with him and play with his judge's paraphernalia. And as I walked out into the sunlight, a huge weight was lifted. I knew that, unlike many people who walk into that courtroom, I had walked out a free man, uncondemned, but, more than that, I had walked out legally and irrevocably connected to the girl in my arms I could now introduce as my daughter. She had a new identity. That meant I had a new identity too – I had become an adoptive father.

Later that night I turned to Romans 8 because I knew I could relate to the part where Paul writes about the agonising wait for adoption. Imagine my surprise when I read again the rest of the chapter. It was as though Paul had been in that courtroom with me:

Therefore, there is now no condemnation for those who are in Christ Jesus, because through Christ Jesus the law of the Spirit who gives life has set you free from the law of sin and death. For what the law was powerless to do because it was weakened by the flesh, God did by sending his own Son in the likeness of sinful flesh to be a sin offering. And so he condemned sin in the flesh, in order that the righteous requirement of the law might be fully met in us, who do not live according to the flesh but according to the Spirit . . .

For those who are led by the Spirit of God are the children of God. The Spirit you received does not make you slaves, so that you live in fear again; rather, the Spirit you received brought about your adoption to sonship. And by him we cry, 'Abba, Father.' The Spirit himself testifies with our spirit that we are God's children. Now if we are children, then we are heirs – heirs of God and co-heirs with Christ, if indeed we share in his sufferings in order that we may also share in his glory.

(Romans 8:1–4, 14–17)

Paul recognises that we are often burdened by self-condemnation, worrying about whether we are measuring up, living in fear, thinking of ourselves as failures, enslaved to the demands and expectations of others, or by our physical appetites and temptations. And he wants us to know that the Spirit of adoption can help us know who we are and celebrate it.

More than justified

The prior seven chapters of Paul's letter to the Romans highlight the fact that all of us are facing charges for which we should be found guilty in God's court of law. We have been caught red-handed. There is incontrovertible evidence against us. There is no excuse and there are no extenuating circumstances. We deserve to feel condemned. But there is a dramatic shift in tone between chapter seven and chapter eight. It is as if the judge has adjourned to the privacy of his chambers to make his deliberations and decide on the sentencing. Then he comes back into the courtroom to declare that, although we are guilty and he has to mete out the full extent of the punishment for our crimes, there is nevertheless to be no condemnation for us, no penalty to pay, no fine to remunerate.

More of us than we might imagine live our Christian lives as though we haven't heard God pronounce us innocent and free to go. Instead we continue to live with a sense of obligation, shame and fear of being caught out. I have seen this insecurity work its way out in very different ways. It makes some of us mean, it makes some of us brash, it makes some of us timid. Being uncertain of our forgiveness and insecure in our identity can have myriad toxic consequences.

Sometimes the fact that God has told us there is

no condemnation ironically seems to induce its own sense of condemnation. Some of us are still trying to earn our way out of that debt as well as attempting to pay back everything else we think we owe for our sins. We may have been convicted, but we are not condemned. We were guilty, but we have been declared righteous. But when that pardon and freedom make us feel guilty, something is terribly wrong. When we punish ourselves even when God is not punishing us, it makes a mockery of God's grace.[5]

Grace is an explosive idea. The unmerited gift of God to humanity has inspired a million songs and much activity. When the Church grasps it, it cannot help but share this incredible gift with the whole world. This amazing truth of justification has been rightly celebrated throughout the history of the Church and around the global Church. It is often regarded as the pinnacle of salvation, the central treasure of the gospel, the end of the story.

But forgiveness is not the end of the story. It is only half the story when it comes to God's amazing grace. The courthouse where God justifies you is the same courtroom where he declares you adopted. When you are declared free, you are also declared family. When you walk out of that building uncondemned and released from guilt and servitude, you also walk out with a new identity. The doctrine of adoption takes the doctrine of justification to a whole deeper level.

When the two are put together, we appreciate both better. It is a double celebration.

J.I. Packer, the world-renowned reformed scholar, agrees:

[Adoption] is the highest privilege that the gospel offers: higher even than justification . . . That justification – by which we mean God's forgiveness of the past together with his acceptance for the future – is the primary and fundamental blessing of the gospel is not in question. Justification is the primary blessing, because it meets our primary spiritual need. We all stand by nature under God's judgment; his law condemns us; guilt gnaws at us, making us restless, miserable, and in our lucid moments afraid; we have no peace in ourselves because we have no peace with our Maker . . . In adoption, God takes us into his family and fellowship – he establishes us as his children and heirs. Closeness, affection and generosity are at the heart of the relationship. To be right with God the Judge is a great thing, but to be loved and cared for by God the Father is a greater.[6]

Imagine a man released from debt. He never wants to see that loan shark again. Imagine a woman reprimanded by the judge for misconduct and sent away to do community service. Despite his kindness, she never wants to cross the judge's path again. Imagine a teenager, caught by a police officer who flushes her drugs down a nearby drain. She knows the officer has risked her job for her, but she still seeks to avoid her for as long as she can. The exchange is complete. The transaction is done. Many of us treat God like this. Our faith may as well be a get-out-of-hell-free card that is stuffed to the back of a drawer or in a subfolder in our email filing system. It is archived and assigned to our history. It is there if we need it, but we are moving on. It becomes a status we can draw on in emergencies rather than the beating heart of who we are. We sense we would do best to avoid God as far as we are able to.

Adoption changes the story and raises the bar. There is not only reprieve, there is also relationship. There is not only freedom from the past, there is also family and a future. There is not only a Judge who makes us right, there is a Father who draws us close, and a Spirit who testifies to our spirit that we are his children, co-heirs with Christ. The family that is the Trinity has included us – legally and irrevocably. There is no condemnation – but there *is* celebration.

Sometimes I think we are like my daughter that day in court. We can be oblivious to what is going on, because someone mentioned ice cream. Our identity, our history, our future, our freedom, our inheritance are all being worked out and we are playing with the gavel. If only we understood the full implications. What God has done means that we are stuck with him forever come what may. By God's grace we are both justified and adopted. Everything has changed.

The trouble is that appropriating our new identity as the forgiven and adopted children of God takes more time than we might realise.

One of my daughter's favourite films is *The Princess Diaries*.[7] It's the story of a teenager living in relative poverty with her single mother. She is a slightly goofy kid and doesn't quite fit in with her peers, and then a limousine turns up at her house and the driver informs her that there's more to her identity than she knows. She is, in fact, the last-surviving heir to the throne of the country of Genovia, a princess who will inherit a magnificent kingdom complete with a picturesque castle, a fortune in wealth and an eligible, handsome prince. The book and the film were wildly popular because this is the dream that many a pre-teen girl harbours. Perhaps this dream taps into a deeper longing, in fact. Perhaps we all secretly long to know that our lives really matter, that we are not just run-of-the-mill clones, that we are more than merely another employee, statistic, or national insurance number. Perhaps we long to know that we are royalty, waiting for our kingdom to appear. And perhaps that longing is not as far-fetched as we might assume.

The bulk of the storyline of the film is dedicated to exploring the culture shock that this young woman from San Francisco finds herself in when she arrives into the European elegance of Genovia. She is the heir to the throne, but she does not know how to live out that identity, and so she must learn what it involves before her coronation takes place. The transition time, between knowing who she is officially and accepting her identity and all it entails, is the interesting part of the story. I feel the same about the Christian life. Christians are a people of great hope. We longingly await our coronation as the sons and daughters – heirs and heiresses – of the King, but how do we live that identity in the meantime, in the time lag? How can we learn the etiquette of the future kingdom, leaving behind the culture and mindset of our past? What if we fail, misunderstand things, and relapse into our old habits? We can be reassured – according to the Spirit of adoption, our destiny is assured. Our performance does not dictate the fulfilment of the promise.

Who am I?

Sometimes people ask my daughter about her biological family. When they refer to them as her 'real family' it can undermine, for her, the reality of her status in my family. Because of adoption she may have to wrestle with the nature-versus-nurture debate to work out who she 'really' is. She may have to work out what it means to belong to two family trees. She may wonder what life would have been like with a different name, different expectations and different values.

Adoption seems to go hand in hand with identity struggles. Adoption forces us to question who we really are, who we really belong to, where we will display our allegiance. This might be good news. For those of us who struggle to embrace our identity as God's children, we can be reassured that, because of our adoption, these internal wrestlings are perfectly normal. So normal, in fact, that God has made a plan to help us. He sends his Spirit of adoption to be a constant help and comfort to us in this. According to Paul in Romans 8, the Spirit of adoption can bring release from the past, encouragement in the present and hope for the future.

I will always feel embarrassed about the photographs of a long-haired bespectacled boy in brown corduroy outfits hanging on the walls in my father's house. I no longer look like the child that I was then. I have changed a lot. But they also give me a peculiar hope. Looking back on the photos reminds me that there is a time lag in my relationship with God too. I still have a long way to go to fully realise my God-given identity. I often get side-tracked by petty insecurities and weighed down by deep, recurring anxieties and feelings of self-condemnation. But all that can change. After all, one day I will have a kingdom to inherit, a celebration to attend, a Family to meet.

As I look forward to that, I take comfort from the words of the courageous Christian martyr Dietrich Bonhoeffer, who was imprisoned and executed for his opposition to the Nazis. He wrote this poem from his prison cell shortly before he was killed:

Who am I? This or the Other?
Am I one person today, and tomorrow another?
Am I both at once? A hypocrite before others,
And before myself a contemptible woebegone weakling?
Or is it something within me still like a beaten
  army
Fleeing in disorder from victory already achieved?
Who am I? They mock me, these lonely questions of
  mine.
Whoever I am, Thou knowest, O God, I am thine![8]

~

Questions for reflection

1. What are the different ways in which we might struggle with our identity? Why is it so difficult for us often to accept that we are God's children?
2. Why does J.I. Packer describe adoption as the highest privilege the gospel offers? How might this challenge your appreciation of your salvation and your identity?

3. Read Bonhoeffer's poem. How does it help you to know that the most inspiring of Christians are not immune to the most fundamental struggles of iden- tity and self-understanding? What peace can you find in his conclusion that God knows exactly who we are, and claims us as his own?

Chapter 3

The secret that changes everything about church

*Why water is thicker than blood —
and chaos more welcome than order.*

A team of scholars and their doctoral students were
sitting in the heat of the African sun listening in rapt
silence to a wise old Kenyan pastor share his story of
how he had become a Christian. With tears running
down his face, he explained his Muslim family's reaction to his conversion, and how he was subsequently
thrown out of his home. Not only that, but when he
refused to recant his confession in Christ he was forced
to flee from his village to save his life. Many miles away
from home, he sought sanctuary in a church building.
The Christian community there welcomed him with
open arms. They gave him a corner of the building to
live in and a mattress on the floor, together with food
generously delivered on a daily basis. The man was
extremely grateful for their protection and hospitality.

I sat with the listening students and scholars, feeling deeply moved by his story and how the tragedy had ended so happily. But the story wasn't finished. It was not a happy ending after all. The pastor continued, confiding that life was tough being, in effect, a refugee. Despite the hospitality of the church, the hardest part of his week was on Sunday morning after the service when everyone went home to their families and their Sunday lunches, leaving him alone in the building with a plate of food to eat by himself. That was when it hit him – he had truly lost everything. Although he was welcome to make his home inside the church building, he was not welcome inside the homes of the church family.

This was no small distinction, I realised. During my own difficult period – by comparison, light and minor – when I struggled to sense God's love and presence, I went to church. I shared the bread and the wine, even with those who meant to do me harm. I closed my eyes during the prayers, lifted my voice during the singing and took notes during the sermons. I got there early to help put out chairs and tables and stayed behind to wash up the coffee mugs. Sometimes I preached. Sometimes I organised youth events. A little like the Kenyan pastor, I was seeking refuge in the church. But true refuge can no more be found in an event than it can in a building. What we were both missing were true, secure, intimate relationships. Church is supposed to be more than an event or a building – church is supposed to be family.

There is an account in Luke's Gospel where Jesus explains this. He has just outlined to a rich young upstart the financial cost of being a disciple. Without apology, Jesus instructed him to sell off all his assets and donate the proceeds to the poor. The disciples balked – that was not a good message for their recruitment drive. Who would choose to follow Jesus with a message as hard as that? But instead of backing down and minimising the challenge of discipleship, Jesus pressed the point home even further. Not only should people expect to lose all their possessions, they might, like my Kenyan friend, lose all their family too. But Jesus made a solemn promise to compensate for that costly sacrifice:

> 'Truly I tell you,' Jesus said to them, 'no one who has left home or wife or brothers or sisters or parents or children for the sake of the kingdom of God will fail to receive many times as much in this age, and in the age to come eternal life.'
>
> (Luke 18:29–30)

According to Jesus, those who convert to Christianity at great relational cost will receive many times more brothers, sisters, parents and children in the here and now. How is this possible? It is through the alternative family of the church that we receive relationships that can act as a substitute for those that we have lost.

But that is not what the Kenyan convert running for his life had experienced. The church building provided shelter, the church members provided sustenance, and the church events provided sacraments and spiritual teaching – but none of these were a substitute for the lifelong, intimate commitment of a family.

It is relatively rare that I meet people like the Kenyan pastor, who have lost family because of conversion to Christianity. However, I meet people every day whose families have been torn apart for other reasons: violence, abuse, mental health crises, poverty, conflict, drugs, war, illness, tragedy. I expect you could tell me your own stories of the terrible impact family breakdown has had on those you know and love. How reassuring it is that Jesus affirms the importance of family – both now and after death. How wonderful that family is not restricted to those who share our DNA. How incredible that Jesus proposes that the church could be involved in the creation of a new intimate, supportive, protective family for those who have lost their natural family.

Jesus portrays the church as an alternative family whose members, despite not being genetically connected, are committed to one another with the same intensity that blood relatives might feel for one another. The church is described as a family formed through covenant and commitment despite different ancestry and parenthood. That sounds a lot like adoption to me.

Church is family

So what does it mean to be a family? When is a family a family? That was a question I had to ask myself when I began fostering. Is it the sharing of a building? Was I connected to my fostered and birth children only when we were under the same roof? Is it the sharing of an activity? Were we only family when we were gathered around the dinner table? Or out on a trip to the beach? Or when I was involved in teaching the little ones to tie their shoelaces, or helping my teenagers understand Shakespeare? Family is more than any of this. It is a 'we' that is bigger than the sum of its 'I' parts. It is a unit even though we are many different members. It is a togetherness even when we are scattered. It is a bond that can exist even when we live on opposite sides of the planet or have only just met. It is a covenant for the future whatever happened in the past. It is a relational entity that moves forward without leaving anyone behind.

Too often we explain the gospel in terms of a personal relationship with God. Although partly true, the emphasis can be misleading. When I adopted my daughter it did not only affect the relationship between her and me. A family that goes from five people to six immediately increases the number of individual relationships from ten to fifteen. And then there are new aunts, uncles, cousins, grandparents. Relationships increase exponentially. The doctrine of adoption teaches us that when we become a Christian, God becomes our Father, Jesus our brother, the Spirit our comforter, and the church becomes the family to which we belong, with all the multitude of relationships that that entails. Because of adoption, the church was never supposed to be just a building, or just an event – it was always supposed to be family.

There is something about a newborn that displays that brilliantly. Each foster baby that arrives in our family quickly makes him or herself at home in church too. From the moment they enter the service they are surrounded by children trying to make them gurgle and smile. When they begin to tire, some kind-hearted soul will scoop them up and soothe them before passing them on to their neighbour, who will forego all their natural inhibitions in order to communicate in baby language, helping them feel safe and valued. By the end of the service the baby has been entertained, fed and winded and is sleeping peacefully in somebody's arms. There is a warmth and a goodwill that intuitively goes out from young and old, rich and poor, male and female as the foster child who is between families is effectively adopted by the family that is the church. But the church benefits just as much. I've seen it in even the most formal and impersonal of churches: the boundaries come down and the baby inspires an intimacy that speaks volumes about the fundamental importance of family connection: acceptance, belonging, commitment.

Unfortunately, a lot of our language presents and reinforces the idea that church is simply an event where religious goods and services are dispensed. We talk about 'going to church'. We hear terms like 'shopping around' for a church, or 'church hopping'. Some Christians are willing to commute long distances to 'attend' a 'brand' of church that 'works' for them. You don't have to look too far to find a pastor frustrated about a new church that has turned up close by, lamenting the number of young people or families who have left to join this latest show in town. But sometimes those same pastors admit that this may, at least in part, be a problem of their own making. Look at any church website and you'll see that what are advertised are worship services for us to enjoy, sermons for us to listen to, youth provision for our children and perhaps a small group that can provide for other needs. We post pictures of our smart buildings, of our edgy youth work and our well-designed sermon series; we invest time and money into brilliant branding and a hip visual identity – thereby to some extent buying into a marketing mindset and promulgating the idea that our churches exist primarily as events for consumer Christians to attend.

Part of the reason for the popularity of the idea that church is an event comes from an oft-quoted definition articulated in the sixteenth-century Augsburg Confession: 'The Church is the congregation of saints, in which the Gospel is rightly taught and the Sacraments are rightly administered.'[1]

This definition was originally formulated while the Protestant Reformation was exploding across Europe, and was worded specifically to exclude the Roman Catholic churches of the time from being seen as genuine churches. For that moment in history it was revolutionary, bravely challenging the errors of the day, helping people to differentiate between authentic and failing churches. But it was a bit like the treasury department's advice regarding bank notes: it is helpful to know that the genuine ones have a watermark and a serial number, but those features do not fully define a bank note, let alone indicate anything of the purpose and function of money. Similarly, the Augsburg Confession's definition may have been helpful in the sixteenth century as a litmus test, but it does not define the purpose or function of the church. Yes, it is important that the Word of God is rightly preached and the sacraments are rightly administered, but there is so much more to church. Misapplying the information only leads to the development of a transactional or consumer model of church.

I believe that Bible teaching and sacraments are an important part of church life in the same way that helping my children with their homework and providing food for them are important parts of family life. But if that was the only way I related to my children you would wonder what kind of parent I was. Or if I were to define parenting as remembering to be there to photograph my child's sports day, piano recital or birthday party, you would probably argue I had a reductionist and limited understanding of parenting. In the same way, we misunderstand church if we only turn up to Sunday services, Bible studies and prayer meetings and exclude the Bible's clear teaching to 'love one another',[2] 'carry each other's burdens',[3] 'encourag[e] one another'[4] and 'spur one another on toward love and good deeds'.[5] These ongoing commitments to the members of our church family don't fit neatly into the confines of a Sunday worship service. Adoption provides us with a new definition of church which locks into our approach to church life commitments of love and belonging, intimacy and family.

Water is thicker than blood

The children in my home, whether mine by birth, fostering or adoption, are all genuinely part of the family as far as I am concerned. They are included in every meal, every family conversation, every holiday, every festival. In my eyes they have equal value, dignity and worth. It does not matter whether they are with us for a few weeks or a few decades; relationally, they all get the same rights and treatment because blood is not thicker than water according to my understanding of the gospel. The water of baptism unites us together as a family in a way that even relativises genetic relationships.

This is what Jesus wanted the world to know when he refused, on one occasion, to speak to his mother Mary and his brothers. He had been interrupted from preaching to the crowd to be told they were standing outside waiting to speak to him, and he replied:

> 'Who is my mother, and who are my brothers?'
> Pointing to his disciples, he said, 'Here are my mother
> and my brothers. For whoever does the will of my
> Father in heaven is my brother and sister and mother.'
> (Matthew 12:48–50)

Jesus, who loved his mother so much that he made provision for her care even on the cross,[6] claims that those who serve God are as important to him as the family who raised him. Jesus, who affirms the Mosaic Law that argued that failing to care for your parents is a crime against the God-given value of family,[7] demonstrates that walking away from those who do the will of God the Father is also a crime against the God-given value of family. Jesus, who promised that we would face persecution, even from family, for our faith, also promises that the church can be a substitute family. Being adopted into the family of God gives us the same rights to access Jesus as the brothers and mother who shared some of his DNA. It also gives us the right to expect the same sense of acceptance, belonging and commitment we should expect to find in a biological family.

The Bible depicts a church community whose members are so committed to one another that it could, if required to do so, replace a genetic family. For example, Paul instructs Timothy that he should treat older women as mothers, younger women as sisters, older men as fathers and younger men as brothers.[8] This is typical of Paul's teaching and example. At the end of the letter to the Romans, Paul sends greetings to the church, asking to be remembered to his 'sister Phoebe' and Rufus's mother, 'who has been a mother to me, too'.[9] There is a depth of intimacy indicated in these greetings that may well have been forged during times of common persecution, as a result of separation from wider biological family, and also out of common courageous service to God in difficult and dangerous times.

We also have common ground with our church family because of our common connection with Christ, and because of our common foundation on God's Word. In Ephesians, Paul declares that there is a transformation that comes from being adopted into God's family:

> *Consequently, you are no longer foreigners and strangers, but fellow citizens with God's people and also members of his household, built on the foundation of the apostles and prophets, with Christ Jesus himself as the chief cornerstone.*
>
> *(Ephesians 2:19–20)*

If we allow adoption to inform our understanding of church, we will recognise that some of the criteria we use for choosing whether to join or stay at a church are not always informed by Scripture. When I go to family gatherings, I don't expect my sister to provide restaurant-standard food, and I don't expect my son to choose a playlist that I would enjoy. I do expect there to be a bit of tension between the crabby uncle and anyone who crosses his path. It will doubtless feel a bit cramped, one of the kids will have a meltdown and we won't have as much fun as the family next door – but there's no way I'd consider leaving my family because of these things, yet I have met many people who use exactly these criteria for leaving churches. I have met people who have left their local church over the diet of teaching provided, over the quality of music on offer, or in favour of the more happening church down the road. This may demonstrate that the bonds of love that tie us together have been disintegrated by the acid of consumerism. If we see the church as our adopted family it will help us to resist that, and re-envision our approach to our communal life as Christians.

The church-as-family metaphor offers a healthy counterbalance to the church-as-event mindset. It can be an antidote to the more individualistic – sadly, even consumptive – models of church participation. Families look out for one another, families are committed to each other for the long haul. Families' bonds are strong and, wherever possible, permanent. They support one another through tragedy and triumph. Families are not making economic calculations about cost and benefit. They are committed for better or worse, for richer and poorer.

Chaos is normal

When I say these sorts of things from the stage at conferences, there will always be a queue of people waiting to speak to me afterwards, and they all say the same thing: 'But you haven't seen *my* church!' I then go on to hear horror stories of churches where the leaders are involved in affairs, where divisions have occurred over the coffee rota, or where satanic forces are allegedly at work against the technology or in the lack of syncopation in the worship band. My heart goes out to them. They remind me of a church I once attended, when I was most in need of the love and support of a church family, but when I saw more conflict, hypocrisy and dissension than I dared believe was possible among those who called themselves God's people.

Adopting my little girl helped me refresh my understanding of church in two ways. First of all, it helped me grasp that because I was adopted by God, the church was automatically my new family. Therefore, our corporate life together is supposed to be marked by a radical and supernatural hospitality, by intimacy, and by a covenant commitment to one another. Second, it helped me understand that just as family is hardly ever straightforward, so in the church, too, there will be complexities, histories and personalities that will necessarily be difficult to work through.

The dynamics of my family when I had two young birth sons is very different to what it is today. Back then, it was relatively simple to make decisions, to take holidays, to manage discipline strategies and treat days. Now I have children in my family who have faced significant amounts of trauma, neglect and abuse. I have children in my family who have disabilities and learning difficulties. One goes into meltdown if something gets dropped. Another can't easily hold a knife and fork or a pen or a toothbrush. One can't cope with noise and crowds. Another can't cope with quiet and predictability. One wants to watch the same cartoons over and over while the other wants to watch new politics documentaries. One wants to do her homework in peace, and another wants to sing at the top of her voice. Our preferences, our needs, our personalities, our talents, our ages are so different that it can make family life pretty chaotic and complicated.

Some adopters don't get this. Many set out to find an easy baby, as close as possible to a perfect child with no baggage, no strings and no complications. Perhaps this baby is supposed to replace the child that they were hoping to have through natural birth. Because of this, both locally and around the world, older children, sibling groups, children from minority ethnic families and those with additional needs or additional trauma wait the longest to find adoptive families. God's adoption of us was very different. God seems to delight in welcoming the most diverse, the most vulnerable, the most chaotic and the most complicated people.

The requirements for being adopted into God's family do not involve power, prestige, perfection, personality or performance. When Paul is reviewing the membership of the Corinthian church, he first acknowledges those who belong to it as his siblings and then notes how God brought them together as family despite their natural disadvantages:

> *Brothers and sisters, think of what you were when you were called. Not many of you were wise by human standards; not many were influential; not many were of noble birth. But God chose the foolish things of the world to shame the wise; God chose the weak things of the world to shame the strong. God chose the lowly things of this world and the despised things – and the things that are not – to nullify the things that are, so that no one may boast before him.*
>
> *(1 Corinthians 1:26–9)*

Because God has offered us welcome and hospitality despite our history, backgrounds and ongoing behaviours, we can expect a degree of chaos and complexity in our churches. Not only should we expect it, we should welcome it. By grace our church families are formed, and grace is to be modelled to one another and to outsiders. The trickier the context, the greater the grace that may be required. But the more conscious we are of our own adoption story, the more likely we are to be patient and hospitable and forbearing with our local church.

Adoption is the secret that changes everything about church. Church is not an event or a transaction or a building or even a community or a religious duty – it is family. As with any adoptive family, we can expect to find not only radical hospitality that is prepared to cross boundaries and overcome obstacles, but a certain amount of chaos. And just as we see time and again on the pages of our Bible, it is in the middle of family chaos that God does the most incredible and beautiful things.

~

Questions for reflection

1. Consider your church: in what ways does it present itself as an event, as a service provider, as a business and as a family?

2. To what extent are you extended family to people in your church? What practical things can you do to invest more deeply into the relationships in your church?

3. 'The more conscious we are of our own adoption story, the more likely we are to be patient and hospitable and forbearing with our local church.' In what ways can you experience this link between God's adoption of you and your involvement in God's family?

Chapter 4

The secret that changes everything about prayer

Fixing broken attachments –
and finding new connections.

Aged five months, the little girl we would go on to adopt would smile when I walked into the room, loudly shout or cry when she needed something and babble happily at her foster brothers and sisters. Three months later, those instincts had suddenly gone. It was heartbreaking to see our once-bubbly little bundle of energy sit expressionless on my lap, eyes glazed over, silent and apparently lost. In the intervening weeks she had gone to stay with a birth relative in an institution in London, which social services and the legal team thought might help the family get the necessary help for them to stay together. I do not know exactly what happened there. I expect she experienced multiple carers. Maybe she took part in experimental therapies. I have no doubt that the damp old building with its leaking ceilings caused her to physically suffer. I assume she felt we had abandoned her. Instead of familiar faces and predictable routine, chaos and anxiety took over and caused something inside of her to shut down. The social worker thought she might never recover.

From the moment we are born we have an instinct to seek the proximity and protection of an adult for survival. We are dependent on the physical and emotional availability of a predictable caregiver to look after us. If that care is not given, particularly when we are under stress, it has a huge influence on how we see ourselves, our world, and the people around us. This idea, now universally accepted, is called 'attachment theory', and it was first recorded by psychologists John Bowlby and Mary Ainsworth as they studied disturbed children in the 1970s.[1] Attachment theory explains something of the distress my adopted daughter experienced in her first year of life, and some of the knock-on effects that has had. Perhaps it seems obvious, but the implications of attachment issues for babies in terms of a lifetime of human relationships and flourishing are profound. As a foster carer, I have seen many times the way that broken and disordered attachment radically impacts the way that children in our care react when we seek to offer them stability and security, love and affection, discipline and comfort.

As a Christian, I have seen the way that broken and disordered attachment can impact our relationship with God, too.[2] Our spiritual life story begins with the chaotic temptations, abuses and consequences of sin, which sometimes seem so appealing and addictive, yet at other times we sense something of how cruel and destructive they are. Then God in his grace and mercy steps in and offers us freedom and a welcome into a new family. This transition from strangers to children, from slaves to heirs, from enemies to family is not a natural one. That is why one of the Holy Spirit's primary tasks is continually to assure our hearts and minds that we really do have the right to address God as Father.

A sacred synergy

Issues stemming from broken attachments take a long time to work through and, for this reason, those considering adopting a child are usually sent for attachment training. The knowledge you get from studying attachment theory can transform your relationship with your adopted child in both the short and the long term. The insights I have gleaned over the years from therapeutically parenting children with attachment issues have also, strangely, transformed the way I understand prayer and my relationship with God.

There are a number of problems and paradoxes that we commonly experience when it comes to prayer. Why, despite an intrinsic desire to pray, do we still find it so difficult? Why do we feel so isolated when God doesn't seem to answer? Why can prayer sometimes bring us great peace, and at other times cause great frustration? Why does it feel like prayer doesn't work most of the time? Doesn't God care about what we want? Or is he just too busy to involve himself in our lives? Is it because my requests are too trivial, or too complex, that God doesn't immediately intervene? Is it because of something I've done, or something I've not done? Is my faith too weak, or my words too few, or my attitudes too unholy?

I believe that our adoption into God's family can be the secret to unlocking not only the untold mystery of prayer but also its untold majesty. Adoption gives us a frame of reference which helps us understand the significance and the struggles of prayer, particularly in a context of relationships that are both fractured and restored, temporary and permanent, stressful and secure. Until we have understood our adoption we will never really make sense of prayer, and until we have understood prayer, we will never really make sense of who we are as adopted children of God. There is a sacred synergy between our prayer life and our adoption.

A new hope

Prayer is one of God's primary mechanisms for deepening and exploring our relationship with him. Prayer is the way that we spend time together, converse together, find comfort, guidance, reassurance. It is the means by which we build trust, intimacy and depth in the strange new relationship in which we find ourselves. It is the safe place, the secure base where our broken attachment with God, together with all of its knock-on effects, can get reordered and repaired.

A powerful starting point given to us by God when it comes to seeing prayer as a way of repairing our attachment to him is the Lord's Prayer. This scripted prayer is difficult for some of us. Perhaps we have recited it so often that it has lost its meaning. It might be that the terminology used does not seem to connect with our own struggles. But when we view it not as a spell, a ritual or a formality, but as a reframing tool given to us by God for our flourishing, perhaps we can access some of its life-changing power. The Lord's Prayer was never supposed to restrict our relationship, it was given to help restore it. Like a parent helping a child find the words to express their deepest feelings, so God here graciously encourages and enables us to begin talking to him about the stuff that really matters – our relationships, our fears, our daily struggles, our temptations, our longings, our future, our identity:

This, then, is how you should pray:
'Our Father in heaven,
hallowed be your name,
your kingdom come,
your will be done,
*   on earth as it is in heaven.*
Give us today our daily bread.
And forgive us our debts,
*   as we also have forgiven our debtors.*
And lead us not into temptation,
but deliver us from the evil one.'

(Matthew 6:9–13)

These words can reshape, reboot and refocus our prayers, offering a rhythm for expressing our own hurts and needs, setting a pace that is neither arduous nor mindless. In the context of the religious teaching of the day, which said prayers had to be showy and wordy, this short and simple example gave hope to those who prayed in secret,[3] who prayed on their knees, who didn't know where to start or what to say. Jesus saw right through the sham and pretence of many religious leaders and offered a model of authenticity and hope for everyone.

There are three main sections to the Lord's Prayer, and each is given a powerful new perspective when we factor in our adoption into God's family. First comes our ability to call God 'Father' and learn where we belong; second is the implication of our new identity and learning how we are accepted; and, third comes the resources we can rely on as we learn when to trust our Father's provision.

A new bond

I will never forget one little boy who turned up on my doorstep wearing his school uniform and carrying just his lunch box and his swimming kit in his hands. He was so full of rage that his face was permanently red and it looked like every muscle in his body was tight and constricted. All he wanted was to be able to go home. But he never did. I found him once on a laptop zooming in on Google Earth desperately trying to find his house. My heart went out to him. He felt so betrayed, displaced. Nine months later, I drove that little boy to a new family who had promised to care for him for the rest of his life. It was a journey we had made frequently over the previous weeks as they had got to know each other. This time would be the last, and now he had significantly more than his swimming kit with him. Surrounded by suitcases full of clothes, a bike, and toys and mementos of his time with us, he was excited and nervous. After a while, having been unusually quiet, he asked me if I thought it would be okay if he called this new family 'Mum and Dad'. That question broke me, especially knowing how much he had longed to go home. We had to drive a bit slower after that, as the road was blurring through my tears.

Helping a child become ready to call someone else Mum and Dad is one of a foster parent's greatest ambitions. For those children who can't go home again, this is the next best thing. To see them overcome the broken attachments in their life so that they are ready to commit and trust again is a major therapeutic goal. The apostle Paul understood something of this. In both of his clearest expositions of the doctrine of adoption he talks about the Holy Spirit's work in preparing us to call God 'Father'. We have already looked at the occasion in Romans when Paul says it is because of the Spirit of adoption that we cry '*Abba*, Father'.[4] Similarly, in Galatians he says it is the Spirit of adoption whom God sent 'into our hearts, the Spirit who calls out, "Abba, Father."'[5] It is no wonder that Jesus begins the Lord's Prayer by encouraging us to address God as our 'Father'.

There are many other names that God uses throughout the Bible as he helps us know him. Jesus could have taught us to address God as Lord, Yahweh, the Almighty, the Most High, the Everlasting One, the great I AM. Compared with the thousands of times God is introduced with these names in the Old Testament, he is referred to as 'Father' only fourteen times.[6] The great patriarchs and prophets Abraham, Moses, Isaiah and David didn't dare to call God

'Father'. But in the New Testament, Jesus commands his disciples to call God this most intimate of all his names. Paul drives home that sense of intimacy with the word 'Abba', which was Jesus' unique, affectionate way of addressing God. Incredibly, Jesus and the Holy Spirit encourage us to share that privilege – because of our adoption. And because of our adoption, we are to share that privilege with others – we address him not as *my* Father but as *our* Father, affirming our attachment both to God and to one another. Because of our adoption we recognise that God is the ultimate standard of fatherhood – he is *our Father in heaven* – far removed from the deficiencies of our earthly parents and far exceeding the beauty of our earthly parents.

A new acceptance

Immediately following the pronouncement in court that I was now a father to the little girl in my arms, I was given a form to fill in. I had filled in many, many forms over the course of becoming an adopter, but this one seemed momentous. There was a small box where I wrote in her new surname. With that I became her father. And she took on the name 'Kandiah'.

Whenever I read or say the Lord's Prayer now, I am reminded of that life-changing little box as I notice the same link: 'Our *Father* in heaven, hallowed be your *name'*. When we get to call God 'Father', his name becomes our name. His honour becomes our honour. This is a momentous truth that deserves more than a moment's reflection.

I remember going on a primary school trip to France. It was only a short trip across the Channel, but it felt like we were going to the ends of the earth. As we sat on the coach dressed in our simple school uniform, bubbling with excitement, our teachers told us that the reputation of our school rested on our behaviour. This was underlined by the fact that our school sweatshirts carrying the insignia 'Fairlight First School' were visible for all to see. The school uniform helped me to feel safe – even in a new country with a strange language I could spot my party and know where I belonged. It helped me to feel proud – I was representing my school on this important occasion. And it helped me behave as I sought to live up to the expectations of the teachers. As the adopted children of God, everywhere we go, we carry our Father's name and reputation. This should give us first of all security, self-esteem and a sense of belonging; and second, it gives us an incentive to live to honour him.

Some Christians think that our prayer for God's name to be honoured is simply a reminder not to blaspheme. But the Lord's Prayer links it with two other petitions showing that there is much more at stake. 'Hallowed be your name' is closely followed by

'Your kingdom come' and 'Your will be done, on earth as it is in heaven.' God's name will be honoured when his will is done. God's kingdom comes as his will is done on earth as it is in heaven. God's will is done when we live mindful of the name and reputation of God that we carry with us.

This connection is corroborated in the rest of the Bible. Each occasion when God explains that his name has been dishonoured clearly stems from the way his people have failed to offer justice and grace to those around them. Here are two examples from Jeremiah and Amos:

But now you have turned around and profaned my name; each of you has taken back the male and female slaves you had set free to go where they wished. You have forced them to become your slaves again.

(Jeremiah 34:16)

They trample on the heads of the poor
as on the dust of the ground
and deny justice to the oppressed.
Father and son use the same girl
and so profane my holy name.

(Amos 2:7)

It is as we seek justice, help the poor, and stand up to abuse that we honour God's name, do God's will and usher in God's kingdom. This is our privilege and our responsibility.

But what happens when we don't?

There have been many times when my children have acted in small ways that undermine the reputation of my name. I remember one of them having a tantrum at a church picnic at the age of three. Another was caught, aged five, carving his name onto his school desk while bored in a lesson. Another got a detention for inappropriate language at the age of twelve. Did any of these incidents ever cause me to retract their name? Of course not. I try to love my children unconditionally, which means that although they experienced unenjoyable consequences for their choices, their place in the family, their name, was never in question.

We are accepted by God unconditionally. God loves us when we honour him. He loves us when we fail him. The prophets Amos and Jeremiah were sent to God's people not to disinherit them of his name, but rather to give them a chance to change, to repent and reconcile with God, to remind them to live up to the name they had been given. Similarly, the Lord's Prayer is not teaching us that we must earn our salvation; rather, Jesus is acknowledging that honouring God's name is not always easy, and we need God's help and grace, and the help and grace of our brothers and sisters. Paul leads by example when he writes this to the church in Thessalonica:

With this in mind, we constantly pray for you, that our God may make you worthy of his calling, and that by his power he may bring to fruition your every desire for goodness and your every deed prompted by faith. We pray this so that the name of our Lord Jesus may be glorified in you, and you in him, according to the grace of our God and the Lord Jesus Christ.

(2 Thessalonians 1:11–12)

A new provision

One boy who came into my care always made us smile at mealtimes. Before the rest of the family had gathered at the table, he would run to his place and heap the lion's share of food onto his plate. I used to tell him: 'Trust me – take your time – there's plenty to go round,' but he just couldn't get past the years of feeling hungry and unprovided for before he came into care. And so he always ate like it was his first-ever meal and, at the same time, could be his last.

Sometimes I see myself in that lad when it comes to my prayer life with God. I want it now. I want it all. I'm not really considerate of everyone else's needs. I don't really trust that God has plenty to go around. I don't really learn from experience that God will provide for me tomorrow, just as he did today and yesterday. I need to hear a kind, gentle voice reassuring me that I can trust God to provide for everything, every day.

The final section of the Lord's Prayer is that voice. It whispers a reminder that our heavenly Father cares for us and will provide for all our needs, for always. All we have to do is ask. Not in a wordy way as though we can verbally bully God into submission.[7] Not in a showy way as though we can manipulate God into thinking we somehow have earned his grace.[8] Not in a spooky way, as though we were uttering a magical spell to force a distant deity to intervene in a world he doesn't care about or know. Not in a desperate way, as though we were fighting a losing cause. Prayer is simply like a child talking to his father. And our Father, who knows our history and our hurts and our hang-ups, graciously listens and graciously provides.

In this final phrase there are four petitions:

Give us today our daily bread.
And forgive us our debts,
    as we also have forgiven our debtors.
And lead us not into temptation,
    But deliver us from the evil one.

                    (Matthew 6:11–13)

Here we see Jesus putting words to our most basic needs: our physical needs, our relational needs, our ethical needs, our spiritual needs. When a child comes into care with an attachment disorder, they require exactly the same things. They need help learning to trust that we will provide for them physically, that we will support them as they work out their relationships, that we will offer them wisdom in their decision-making, and that we will support their spiritual development too. We don't expect them to tell us to do these things, we just do them anyway. But as they put into words their wants and needs, as they accept, and as they seek out our input, this builds a deepening trust over time.

Another child we cared for used to hide in the furthest corner of the house. When we would go and sit with him he would relocate to a different isolated spot. His experience of adults had taught him to avoid them at all costs. One day the little boy appeared in the kitchen. The vehicle he had been playing with had broken. I fixed it for him and off he went. Five minutes later he returned and held up the vehicle again for me to fix. This happened about ten times before a guest in the house got a little exasperated and suggested that I should throw it away and give him a different toy. I smiled and explained with a tear in my eye that the broken car may just have been the best gift he could hope for. Every time he asked for help, it reinforced that here was an adult whom he could trust, who would welcome him, listen to him and help him as best he could.

When we put ourselves in the shoes of an adopted child learning to trust a good father who is desperate to provide the world for them, we see that prayer is not just a task to be done or an order to be obeyed, it is a lifeline to the most safe and permanent relationship we could ever wish for. Communication with God, even of the most repetitive sort, can help begin to rewire our brain, overcome the hurts of the past and build an intimacy into the future.

I prayed a lot for that little girl who sat expressionless on my lap, her eyes glazed over, silent and apparently lost. She is a teenager now. She is bubbly and outgoing, and when she walks into any room she is very happy to be the centre of attention. Because of her history there are ongoing challenges in her life, things that she struggles to grasp about who she is, behaviour that she struggles to manage. And so, even though she has come so far, I continue to pray for her to become a confident young woman, make her mark on the world and know her Father God's comfort, challenge and compassion. Every time I pray for her I am challenged to remember my Father's listening ear when we pray, his attentiveness to our cries and his awareness of our longings.

The Spirit of adoption can do that for you. He can burst your prayer life out of the formalities. He can ground your prayer life in the reality of all your needs and all your weaknesses. He can fuel your prayer life as your eyes are opened to the needs of those around you. He can shift your prayer life gradually so that you start to seek God's glory and his kingdom rather than your own comfort and agenda. And he can bond you with the Father who loves you, helping you know his security, compassion and provision. As the Spirit of adoption changes your prayer life, you may just find that he changes you and those you love too.

~

Questions for reflection

1. What difficulties relating to attachment have you experienced, and how may those impact your relationship with your Father God?

2. Which of the three fostered children described in this chapter do you relate to most spiritually – the one who had to come to terms with a new 'dad', the one who was learning to trust he would be provided for physically, or the one for whom broken things led to a closer bond with the one who could fix things? How could prayer help you to trust that God will provide for your spiritual, physical and relational needs?

3. How could listening to the Spirit of adoption transform your prayer life?

Chapter 5

The secret that changes everything about mission

The missionary myth –
and where we go from here.

Since the age of fifteen, when I became a Christian, I wanted to become a missionary. I had a world map on my wall and at night would dream about where God would send me. As I got older, I would spend Saturdays combing the shelves of my local Christian bookshop and devouring compelling stories of missionaries such as Jim Elliot in Ecuador, Hudson Taylor in China and Amy Carmichael in India. That was until I managed to secure a Saturday job opening envelopes for American Express, which then gave me the opportunity to help raise funds to go on short-term mission trips in my summer holidays. By the time I had my sixth-form meeting with the school careers advisor my CV was ready: I could now finalise steps to become a lifelong missionary.

A few months later I went to a Christian missions conference and everything changed. The room was packed full of eager young women and men who wanted to serve God across the planet. The keynote speaker launched into the grand finale of the confer- ence and asked us to stand up if we met any of the following criteria:

Number one: can you speak a foreign language fluently? I guessed my GCSE French and the random Tamil slang words my cousins had taught me didn't count. I stayed in my seat.

Number two: can you repair a car? I was surprised by how many other people stood up at this point. My own engineering skills were exhausted by opening the bonnet of the car and breathing in deeply through my teeth.

Number three: are you good with children? Well, I had been one for most of my life, but I didn't think that was what they were looking for. I didn't move.

Number four: do you have IT skills? I was pretty nifty with a Word document and not bad at Microsoft Paint. But building IT infrastructure, networking, programming, not so much. Still sat down.

Number five: are you great at administration? Seriously? My ability to administrate my life was limited: it was a miracle when I made it to lectures and submitted my coursework on time. I was always running out of milk and clean socks. I didn't think my 'administration skills' were something the mission field would appreciate. Never mind. I had one more chance.

And finally – can you drive a car? Er, no. Driving lessons were an expensive luxury that was out of reach for my family.

Everyone in the room had stood up. Except me. Everyone in the room was then prayed for as they anticipated their exciting futures as missionaries. Except me. Everyone went home from the conference buzzing. Except me.

My friends back on my university campus thought I had had a lucky escape. They seemed to imagine God as a reality TV show producer recruiting cross-cultural missionaries and subjecting them to maximum discomfort and embarrassment. In their eyes God seemed to deliberately send people to inhospitable places and get them to eat foods that would make them retch purely for his own personal entertainment. They thought they could hang out with me more now that they weren't always expecting me to start preaching to every stranger I met and manipulating conversations towards a 'Jesus punchline'.

My romantic bubble of missionary dreams had been well and truly burst, and I was left wondering not only what I would do with my life but also what I would do with my faith. It wasn't until years later that I finally realised that the missions conference keynote speaker had got mission pretty wrong. By then I had also understood that many other Christians get mission all wrong too. Some seem to think mission is only mission if you live in a hut in Africa. Others think mission is only mission if you have to go round asking for financial support and giving out prayer letters. Some of us seem to live with a continual sense of panic that the fate of the world rests on our shoulders, while others of us are so relaxed with the idea that God will do everything himself that we just get on pursuing the same dreams and ambitions we had before we became Christians.

My mildly traumatic experience at that student missions conference may have been one of the reasons I ended up investing ten years of my life in academic study and teaching in the area of missiology. But, like so much in the Christian life, it turns out that our understanding of mission might be given a significant head start by tuning into the Spirit of adoption.

The beginning of mission

As a young person, I was taught that the first mention of mission in the Bible comes in the Great Commission at the end of Matthew's Gospel, when Jesus tells his disciples to go to the ends of the earth and make more disciples. For a long time, it was not only my starting point for understanding mission

– it was my entire understanding of mission. Then I heard a sermon suggesting that mission in the Bible began a lot earlier – way back in the opening chapter of Genesis. That's when the penny dropped. The whole Bible is the story of the mission of God,[1] what he is doing in the universe. Mission is not what we do *for* God, it is what we do *with* God. (As, by the way, the Great Commission confirms, on closer inspection.)

A simple way to break down what God is doing in the universe is by seeing it in terms of four relationships:[2]

1. **The *us-and-God* relationship**: God created human beings in his image so that we would reflect his character to a watching universe.
2. **The *us-and-others* relationship**: God created human beings with an inbuilt need for one another so that together we might build families, communities, nations, companies and systems that would honour him by caring for one another.
3. **The *us-and-our-world* relationship**: God created a place for human beings to explore, nurture and cultivate together.
4. **The *us-and-ourselves* relationship**: God created human beings to be reflective and self-aware and able to cultivate an inner life that could honour him too.

We can find all these relationships perfectly in sync in Genesis 1 and 2, and all these relationships severely fractured by the fall in Genesis 3. The rest of the Bible tells the story of God's mission to restore and reconcile all of these fractured relationships and of how God is superintending history so that, one day, they will all be repaired and renewed. The end of the book of Revelation shows us a beautiful picture of the four restored relationships – *us-and-our-world*, *us-and-God*, *us-and-others* and *us-and-ourselves*:

> *Then I saw 'a new heaven and a new earth,' for the first heaven and the first earth had passed away, and there was no longer any sea. I saw the Holy City, the new Jerusalem, coming down out of heaven from God, prepared as a bride beautifully dressed for her husband. And I heard a loud voice from the throne saying, 'Look! God's dwelling place is now among the people, and he will dwell with them. They will be his people, and God himself will be with them and be their God. "He will wipe every tear from their eyes. There will be no more death" or mourning or crying or pain, for the old order of things has passed away.'*
>
> *He who was seated on the throne said, 'I am making everything new!' Then he said, 'Write this down, for these words are trustworthy and true.'*
> *He said to me: 'It is done. I am the Alpha and the Omega, the Beginning and the End. To the thirsty I will*

give water without cost from the spring of the water of life. Those who are victorious will inherit all this, and I will be their God and they will be my children.'

(Revelation 21:1–7)

God's mission is to repair all four of the fractured relationships, and here in Revelation he paints this majestic picture of his end goal that culminates in his intention to live as an adopted family: *they will be my children.* In other words, if the whole story of the Bible can be summarised by this journey to restore relationships from the original family to God's ultimate family, then understanding the goal of adoption and the lens of adoption should help us enormously as we seek to serve God in the world today.

Us-and-God: adoption of humanity

When my wife and I understood the need our foster daughter was in, there was no doubt or hesitation in our minds that adoption was the best thing we could give her. Adoption was the way we could commit to taking full account of her needs in a lifelong intimate and loving relationship where she would be safe to grow and flourish. She didn't just need money and food and education and opportunity – she needed us. In one sense we were the best gift we could give to her. When God sees humanity's need he recognises that *he* is the best thing that he could give to us. God expresses this in all sorts of ways in the grand Bible narrative. God comes to Moses and, before he commissions him, he wants him to know who *he* is, revealing himself at the burning bush as 'I am'. God could easily have led his people to the Promised Land in a few days, but he eked it out over a few decades, because the most important thing was to build that bond with him – *he* would protect and provide for his vulnerable children. *He* was there in the fire, the cloud, the water, the rock. He wanted them to rely on *his* provision of food in the desert so that they would know we don't live by bread alone but by the promised provision of God.[3] God could have sent Jesus on a much shorter-term mission to die for the sins of the world, but first he sent Jesus to live with us, because being with God is the whole point of our salvation. God wants us to know that *he* is the best thing he could give to us. That Father–child relationship is the root of his mission, just like Christ is the root of Christianity. We are doing mission when we recognise that it is all about who he is, how we are with him and how we point others to him.

Us-and-others: adoption into a family

I have lost count of the number of times people have asked me what impact each adoption has had on my other children. This question quite rightly stems from the recognition that adoption changes every relationship within the family. If you don't think about it before you adopt a child, you will certainly think about it afterwards. Every day involves guiding each of our children through the positive and challenging interactions with one another. In the same way, God's mission in adopting humanity necessarily involves creating a family, with all the complex relationships with one another that entails. I love that the Bible shows this so honestly. From Adam and Eve struggling to parent two very different children, to Noah's dysfunctional family, to Abraham being tempted to idolise his long-awaited child and disinherit his surrogate child, to Jacob's complex family dynamics with children from different mothers. I could go on through most of the families of the Old Testament. In the New Testament, church families are presented as being equally challenging, with jealousy, arguments, idolatry and affairs. God knows that it is difficult for us to get on with one another, but it is his mission to guide us through our relationships because he is committed to building his family: a family that will be so diverse it could be compared to a great city, and yet be so integrated and unified that it displays the beauty befitting the perfect bride of Christ.

God's mission is our mission when we are adopted into his family and are working out the adopting grace and love of God in our relationships with others. Whether it is the way we treat our neighbours and our politicians, our colleagues and our teammates, friends and family, strangers and enemies, as Christians we are called to be part of God's irresistible revolution of love and to treat everyone as though they are, or one day may be, our brothers and sisters. We are doing mission when we are learning to love our neighbours as ourselves, sharing our food with those who are hungry, seeking the welfare of the city, speaking up on behalf of vulnerable people, patiently supporting dysfunctional families, building just and equitable systems, institutions and companies[4] infused with grace and mercy, and loving one another as Christ has loved us.

Us-and-our-world: adoption and a home for good

When we were first turned down for adoption it was because the social worker who answered the phone to our initial inquiry thought we did not have enough space in our home. We argued that it did not matter if we did not have much space in our home, because the important thing was that a child had space in our hearts, but she was having none of it. So we moved house. Now there was space – a whole extra bedroom. It ticked a box for a social worker. But that space gave me an idea. This would not just be any old space. I put up a cot. I hung a mobile, I chose soft furnishings. I filled the wardrobes with clothes, the shelves with books, and boxes with toys. This was not just a tick box for a social worker – it was a beautiful environment that would make any child smile. And it was not just any old beautiful environment – it was to be *my daughter's* beautiful environment – *her* world, *her* home. The provision of this 'space' and these things was a mark of our love for her before we even met her. As we created her room, we envisioned her enjoying it all, interacting with the different elements, and even adding to it – photos that we would take of her, paintings that she would make, Lego structures she would build, the odd handprint she would add to the paintwork.

God's nursery for humanity was far grander. He painted the walls with trees and flowers and chose ambient lighting that could appear in all different colours. He hung stars in the sky, and he hid gold in the mountains and onyx in the rivers. He brought us real live animals to pet and nurture. God gave us this environment – our world, our home – so that we could enjoy it and flourish in it, and he commanded us to take care of it and make something wonderful out of it. Even though the effects of the fall mean that the world is broken and damaged, the cultural mandate still stands: 'fill the earth and subdue it. Rule over the fish in the sea and the birds in the sky and over every living creature that moves on the ground.'[5] We are called to 'make something of the world'[6] that God has given us stewardship over. In other words, God's mission to restore the world is our mission too.

Personally, I found that when I adopted my daughter and rediscovered my relationship as an adopted child of God, the world looked different. When I saw what a difference I could make to one child, I also saw the huge need for the hundreds of other children in the care system lacking not only a family where they belonged, but a place they could call home. The Spirit of adoption kept putting this need on my heart, and it eventually led to the founding of the adoption and fostering charity 'Home for Good'.[7] But it didn't end there either. Although we are working closely with churches and local authorities to find homes for all the children in the UK who need one, what about the children in other countries in the world? What about children in orphanages, where nobody is even trying to find homes for them? I am a man with a mission as I seek to play a small part in making the world a better place.

Us-and-ourselves: the adoption condition

Stuck to my daughter's mirror is a Bible text that she chose to buy at a Christian festival. It quotes the words from Psalm 139: 'fearfully and wonderfully made'. It is a message I want her to take to heart in a culture that says that unless you look a certain way and dress a certain way, you have little or no value. It is a message I want her to remember when her so-called friends tell her she is too tall, too fat, too loud. When they tell her she is a waste of space, I want her to know that she has inherent dignity and worth. When they tell her that her adoption means that she was unwanted and unloved, I tell her that her adoption means precisely the opposite: she has twice as many parents as her peers have, and two of them chose her specifically.

Thank goodness for the Holy Spirit, who can do a much better job than me at comforting her and confirming to her that her adoption is not a dirty secret to be ashamed of, but a powerful visual aid to the meaning of the universe. Her life path is planned, her forgiveness effective, her status in God's sight secure. Thank goodness for the Bible that shows us that, because of the fall, it is normal for us to feel insecure about our bodies, to feel miserable when people put us down, to feel broken and frustrated when we do things wrong.

Thank goodness for the affirming truths of the Bible, too. God loves us – even when we fail. God wants us even when nobody else does. God can renew our hearts and our minds and one day will renew our bodies too. God's mission to speak truth, to comfort, to affirm our secure adoption is our mission too.

The problem is that those promises in the Bible are sometimes difficult for us to hear and grasp. Sometimes we are so desperate to know them for ourselves that we keep them to ourselves. Sometimes we are far more comfortable applying biblical blessings to ourselves and biblical curses to others. Yet, think of the difference it would make to our world if it were no secret that we are each fearfully and wonderfully made. I meet people every day who have grown up being told the opposite – that they are worthless and useless, that they are a waste of space and a drain on society. Too many people grow up feeling that they are unloved and unwanted, treated as though they were unworthy of even basic care and attention. From what I have learned about therapeutic parenting, I know the messages of love and acceptance and affirmation are not just something adopted children need to hear. An essential component of God's mission – and therefore our mission – is to let the world know that he loved us enough to send his son to die in our place so that we can be called children of God.

We don't need to be able to drive to be able to guide people to a life-changing relationship with God who wants to be their Father. We don't need to be able to fix a car to be able to fix relationships, look out for our neighbours and forgive our enemies – and our friends. We don't need to have good computer skills to get involved in programmes that will make the world a better place. And we certainly don't need a foreign language to speak grace and dignity into the lives of people we meet. Wherever we are, wherever we go, whatever we do, we can join in with God's mission to let everyone know the secret that changes everything – God is in the business of restoring relationships and preparing the world for the ultimate adoption celebration.

~

Questions for reflection

1. Recall the four dimensions of mission. How do they help us to understand our calling as Christian disciples?
2. To what extent are we already involved in mission according to this framework of understanding?
3. What else could we do to help those around us see, know and understand God's plan for the universe? Pray that the Spirit of adoption would speak to you now.

Chapter 6

The secret that changes everything about the Bible

*The greatest story never told –
and how to be part of the happily ever after.*

Perhaps you know the story of a little boy and his sister who are removed from their parents because of domestic violence and, eventually, adopted. But not together. Like so many children in care, they have to be separated because very few adopters are willing to take a sibling group. The little girl is raised in a well-to-do family, while her brother finds himself in the middle of nowhere in the back of beyond. When she grows up, the girl enters public service as she wants to give something back to society. The boy ends up, as is so often the case for care leavers, in the military – a place of structure, belonging and clear-cut social rules. One day they will be reunited. And one day the boy will end up saving not just himself, but his whole squadron. He will be recognised not just as a national hero, but as a global one.

This all took place a long time ago in a galaxy far, far away . . . to a boy called Luke Skywalker.

I have always loved films and like to think of myself as a bit of a film buff. I am a regular at my local cinema half-price-Tuesday-night showings, and it has been known for me, on occasion, to watch three films in one day. But when I adopted my daughter everything changed. I don't mean it curtailed my hobby – in fact, she gave me a fresh excuse to watch old movies again and new Disney movies as they were released. No, everything changed because suddenly I saw themes around adoption cropping up all over the place. This opened up a whole new world of cinematographic engagement.

My blog at the time began filling up with reviews of films and explanations of how, as a Christian and an adoptive father, they helped my understanding of adoption practice and theology, and how, as a charity founder, they helped me promote adoption. A film critic friend of mine, Martin Saunders, used to tell me off. He thought I was seeing things, twisting things, reading my agenda into the narratives. Then, after seeing *The Lego Batman Movie*, the penny dropped for him too and he published a very public apology to me, stating: 'Well, it turns out Krish was right. There is a huge concentration of cinematic story time being given over to one idea: the theme of adoption.'[1]

A eureka moment

Think about it next time you go to watch a film. Chances are if there are children (or young animals or fish) featured, one of them has lost their family or will find a new one – think about Snow White, Bambi, Simba, Tarzan, Anna and Elsa, Nemo, and the protagonists in almost every other Disney film you can think of. Chances are if there are flawed heroes involved, their backstory involves them having lost or gained significant family members. Let's take the major movie franchises of recent decades: Luke and Leia Skywalker were adopted, as we have seen. Superman was adopted. Spiderman was brought up by his aunt. Frodo Baggins was an orphan and brought up by his uncle. Harry Potter was fostered (terribly) by the Dursleys. Paddington lived in supported lodging. James Bond was adopted. Batman was orphaned and brought up by his butler. The list goes on and on.

You see, our screenwriters, authors, playwrights and television producers know that the secret to a good story is a good adoption journey. They know that children who have had the most unimaginably difficult starts in life are the very ones who can develop and portray the resilience and skills they need to make unimaginable successes of life. They know that our families can, paradoxically, cause the deepest of wounds and bring the deepest healing. They know that someone's history does not dictate their destiny. And they know that this storyline seems to connect universally with viewers at a profound, perhaps even spiritual, level.

When I became an adoptive father, I had a eureka moment. I had been let in on entertainment's greatest secret that meant no film would ever be the same again. I had exactly the same experience at the same time in the same way with the Bible. Suddenly I was seeing adoption all over the place. At first, like my friend Martin, I was sceptical. Was I just seeing and twisting things? Was I just projecting my own agenda on to the texts? I decided to delve a bit deeper. But then something happened to me. It's an occupational hazard for every Christian: God spoke to me through his Word. I realised that adoption themes are not simply strewn throughout the Bible – adoption lies at the heart of everything.

A central storyline

At first it was the obvious parts. The three times that Paul describes our adoption into God's family he portrays it as the highest privilege of our salvation, involving all three members of the Trinity in a divine, cosmic, eternal plan. He begins his letter to the Ephesians, for example, with the declaration:

> *Praise be to the God and Father of our Lord Jesus Christ, who has blessed us in the heavenly realms with every spiritual blessing in Christ. For he chose us in him before the creation of the world to be holy and blameless in his sight. In love he predestined us for adoption to sonship through Jesus Christ, in accordance with his pleasure and will – to the praise of his glorious grace, which he has freely given us in the One he loves.*
>
> *(Ephesians 1:3–6)*

This was a major clue as to the absolute importance of adoption to the central storyline of the Bible. But why, if this was the ultimate plan for us, stemming back to before the creation of the world, is it hardly mentioned in the Old Testament?

Just because a term is not used widely in the Bible, it does not mean the theme is not present all the way through. For example, the word 'Trinity' does not appear at all in the Bible, and yet once you have read the New Testament description of God the Father, God the Son and God the Holy Spirit it is virtually impossible to read any part of the Bible without seeing hints of the Trinity. The same is true with adoption. The term is not used in the Old Testament and yet the theme is latent throughout the whole storyline.

The Bible begins with God's corporate family decision to 'make mankind in our image, in our likeness'.[2] Then we read on, seeing God's Spirit at work, foundations being laid that point to Jesus and his mission, and the overarching sovereignty and protection of God the Father. Three mysterious visitors call on Abraham, wisdom is strangely personified in the book of Proverbs, and David glimpses a conversation between his Lord and the Lord.[3] God is a family. God creates a family. And God intervenes to care for dysfunctional families, orphans and widows, ultimately bringing it all together with the adoption into his ultimate family.

Like a melody resonating throughout a symphony, once we begin to understand adoption as the goal towards which God is orchestrating the universe, we should not be surprised to find the theme recurring throughout the Bible in all sorts of different ways.

An orphan turnaround

Perhaps the best place to start is the adoption of the Hebrew child Moses by the daughter of Israel's most feared and oppressive enemy. Moses should have been terminated at birth in Pharaoh's cull, but instead he becomes the greatest human hero in the Old Testament. Moses, the Jews' Jew, the national treasure, was not raised by his birth parents Jochebed and Amram, not because of any fault or deficiency in them, but due to the brutal slavery, oppression and attempted genocide brought about by the Egyptian regime. I love this story and tell it to my daughter often. I find great hope that God can take someone with a traumatic childhood and turn them into a liberator of his people. God saw the child relinquished by his birth mother and hidden in bulrushes and offered him unsurpassed face-to-face access to himself such that the boy's face shone with the reflected Shekinah glory of God. God chose the rescued child to be the one to rescue God's children from captivity. God commissioned the 'orphan' whom the Egyptian princess had found crying to take his law to his people – a law that includes the command:

> *Do not take advantage of the widow or the fatherless. If you do and they cry out to me, I will certainly hear their cry.*
>
> *(Exodus 22:22–3)*

There are over forty occasions where the Bible refers specifically to God's concern for orphans or the 'fatherless'. That's more than the number of times Scripture talks about tithing or taking communion. God makes it clear throughout the Bible that he is particularly interested in the care of vulnerable children. Over and over in the Law revealed through Moses, God reiterates his concern for those who are vulnerable and marginalised:

> *For the Lord your God is God of gods and Lord of*
> *lords, the great God, mighty and awesome, who shows*
> *no partiality and accepts no bribes. He defends the*
> *cause of the fatherless and the widow, and loves the*
> *foreigner residing among you, giving them food and*
> *clothing.*
>
> *(Deuteronomy 10:17–18)*

> *Do not deprive the foreigner or the fatherless of justice,*
> *or take the cloak of the widow as a pledge.*
>
> *(Deuteronomy 24:17)*

> *Cursed is anyone who withholds justice from the foreigner,*
> *the fatherless or the widow.*
>
> *(Deuteronomy 27:19)*

A Father to the fatherless

It is not just in the Old Testament Law that God shows his concern for vulnerable children. It is visible throughout the prophets, in the book of Job and in the Psalms. On one occasion King David is inspired to write:

> *A father to the fatherless, a defender of widows,*
> *is God in his holy dwelling.*
> *God sets the lonely in families,*
> *he leads out the prisoners with singing.*
>
> *(Psalm 68:5–6)*

How does someone become a father to someone else's child? How does God set the lonely in families? Surely David is talking about adoption. And David knew a bit about that. He had come from a large family with six older brothers and two sisters. We are given a clue that things were not always easy in this family when the prophet Samuel comes to visit David's father Jesse to anoint one of his sons. Like Cinderella, not considered worthy enough to be summoned from the cellar when the prince is searching for the belle of the ball, David is not considered important enough to be brought in from the fields. When David was sixteen years old, he had to leave his family behind to begin his new job singing and fighting for King Saul. He struck up a friendship with Saul's son Jonathan, but this relationship was to be wrenched away from him too. Intensely jealous of David, King Saul banished him. David then spent around fifteen years in exile, and many of the psalms are heartfelt cries of loneliness and distress from this period of his life. But God had not forgotten David – eventually he did become king and have his own family. But David never forgot the truth that God sets the lonely in families. He had experienced it for himself; now he felt it was his turn to pass on the blessing.

Remembering his valued friendship with Jonathan, David asked around about what happened to his family after Jonathan had been killed in battle, and when he found out that there was one dependent son left, he effectively adopted him. Mephibosheth had been orphaned and crippled at the age of five, but his emotional scars and permanent physical disabilities were no obstacle to David's love. He provided for him not only financially, but treated him like a son, ensuring that he always joined him at mealtimes. A mighty king using his power and influence to set the lonely in families – this was what David knew about God and what David loved about God, what filled David's lyrics and what filled David's home.

It is argued that because of the complexity of land inheritance rights in Jewish law, there is no legal provision for adoption in the Old Testament.[4] But David finds a way around this when he commands that Saul's land be restored to Mephibosheth, and that Saul's servants are to farm it and bring in the crops. On top of that he gives Mephibosheth a permanent place at his table – a fact that is mentioned four times in seven verses. As this was a privilege usually reserved for the king's sons, it seems that this was the clearest way that David could announce publicly that this boy was to be forever considered family.

An adoption relationship

Just as the two greatest Old Testament heroes – Moses and David – have their adoption journeys, so God also gave the two greatest heroines in the Old

Testament – Esther and Ruth – an understanding of what it meant to be adopted.

The relationship between Esther and Mordecai is one of the most beautiful in Scripture and one that I aspire to in my relationship with my adopted daughter. Mordecai is the model of faithful resistance willing to face death for his love for God, his people and his adopted daughter. Esther is a model of faithful resistance too, willing to risk death for her love for God, his people and her adoptive father. Together they spur each other on to courageous and patient endurance and become the means through which the Jews are saved from genocide.

The book of Ruth is infused with adoption themes. There is the moment when Ruth vows lifelong commitment to Naomi. And Naomi is also presented as a kind of orphan, having lost all her family members, and is then set by God in a family. Boaz goes to court to prove his intention to be the kinsman-redeemer for Ruth. And later, when Ruth and Boaz present their son to Naomi, she prays a blessing over the child that is reminiscent of adoption promises.[5]

When I was younger I read the Bible through from cover to cover in a year by reading three chapters of the Old Testament and a chapter of the New Testament each day. I did this several times, but somehow even then I didn't pick up on God's concern for or prioritisation of the vulnerable. I think I had subtly assumed a filter and subconsciously screened out the parts of the Bible that I didn't think were relevant. Once that filter was lifted, the whole Bible suddenly looked very different.

In Romans 9, Paul describes the whole history of the Israelite nation – in other words, the majority of the Old Testament – as an adoption story:

> *For I could wish that I myself were cursed and cut off from Christ for the sake of my people, those of my own race, the people of Israel. Theirs is the adoption to sonship; theirs the divine glory, the covenants, the receiving of the law, the temple worship and the promises.*
> *(Romans 9:3–4)*

Paul explains that the only way the chosen people of God can claim to be God's children is through adoption. He then shows how all of God's people are part of that story (the New Testament part) through God's mercy. Paul quotes Hosea, who argues:

> *Yet the Israelites will be like the sand on the seashore, which cannot be measured or counted. In the place where it was said to them, 'You are not my people,' they will be called 'children of the living God.'*
> *(Hosea 1:10)*

This is an adoption pronouncement. It is only because of adoption that anyone can be 'called' or counted as somebody else's child. John entreats us to grasp the incredible significance of this when he writes:

> *See what great love the Father has lavished on us, that we should be called children of God! And that is what we are!*
>
> *(1 John 3:1)*

I could give you many, many other examples of how, throughout the Bible, God calls us his children, shows himself to be a Father to the fatherless, sets the lonely in families and includes people who were not his people into his family.[6] But I think it is better that I leave them hidden in the Bible for you to discover for yourself. As you discover the secret that the Bible can be seen as a collection of adoption stories that point to The Great Adoption Story, I hope that you will hear the melody in the symphony of your own Bible study.

A Hollywood ending?

There is an occupational hazard that comes with reading the Bible. It might change us. Eugene H. Peterson, the esteemed theologian and author of the best-selling translation of the Bible into contemporary language, *The Message*,[7] explained why he was so committed to the teaching and explanation of Scripture when he wrote:

Christians don't simply learn or study or use Scripture;
we assimilate it, take it into our lives in such a way that
it gets metabolized into acts of love, cups of cold water,
missions into all the world, healing, evangelism and justice
in Jesus' name, hands raised in adoration of the Father,
feet washed in company with the Son.[8]

When you read, discover and assimilate the biblical threads of God's plan for adoption, God's heart for adoption and God's Spirit of adoption, they might just be metabolised into an adoption story of your own. They might lead you, like David or Mordecai, to reach out to adopt someone into your family.

Adoption of vulnerable children does not come with a promise of a happily ever after ending, despite what the entertainment industry would have us believe. There isn't always a big show-stopping song-and-dance routine as the looked-after child gets adopted by a billionaire, like Annie in the musical named after her. There isn't a guaranteed international showdown as three orphaned girls manage to turn super-villains, like Felonius Gru in *Despicable Me*, into model fathers. Children who have been placed in families by social services may be more likely to find themselves in Her Majesty's Prison Service[9] than in Her Majesty's Secret Service like James Bond. Neither does the Bible promise that our adoption into God's family will be a rose-tinted fairy tale where we become heroes riding off into a Disneyesque sunset. But when we read the biblical accounts of both earthly and heavenly adoption we are given something much more substantial, much more audacious – and much more wonderful.

The same Jesus who promised we would not be left as orphans, but would one day be brought safely to his Father's many-roomed house, also warned us of the troubles we would face in this world.[10] The same Jesus who warned us against misunderstanding our salvation at the final judgment also urges us to pass on God's compassionate grace to the most vulnerable in our communities.[11] The Bible is full of hope and realism, beauty and brokenness, mourning and dancing, comfort and challenge, transformation and frustration, trauma and triumph. Just as we know the reality of that in our own experience of being Christians, adopted into God's family, so too we see that in the adoption of children into our earthly families. And for those of us fortunate enough to experience the two stories side by side, we learn that, as each one informs, impacts and inspires the other, we are helped to live and share our ultimate hope of the truly happily forever after ending the Bible promises.

~

Questions for reflection

1. Think of the last five films you have seen or novels you have read. What adoption themes have they included?

2. 'The Bible can be seen as a collection of adoption stories that point to The Great Adoption Story.' Which passages of Scripture are most radically reframed for you by the adoption plot line of the Bible?

3. What difference could it make in the world if the Church assimilated something of God's plan for adoption, God's heart for adoption and God's Spirit of adoption?

Chapter 7

The secret that changes everything about worship

Doing right things wrong –
and putting wrong things right.

My daughter has a rebellious streak. When I ask her to walk, she runs. When I ask her to run, she walks. When I ask her to be quiet, all sorts of information bursts out of her. When I ask her to talk to me, her mind suddenly goes blank and she has nothing to say. On a good day, I admire her confidence, her guts to do things her own way: it might help her make her unique mark on the world. On a bad day, I worry that it might end her up in a lot of trouble – and I think I might explode with frustration. It is very often the case that the latter reaction is provoked when my camera is involved. You see, my daughter is beautiful – she has long curly hair, sparkling eyes, and a smile that lights up a room. People stop me in the street to tell me how stunning she is. Her phone full of selfies tells me she knows exactly how to pose for a picture. But when *my* camera comes out and I ask her to stand still and smile, she does the exact opposite. It is hard enough trying to get family photographs with seven children facing the same direction. But when one of them is constantly squirming and scowling, it makes the already difficult task virtually impossible. The frustration rises up within me.

Ironically, I can be just like my daughter. Not when it comes to cameras, but at church services. Sometimes if a worship leader stands at the front of the church and tells me to stand, smile and sing, or kneel, confess and pray, or even greet my neighbour with a handshake, something inside me just wants to rebel and do the exact opposite. Telling me how to join in corporate worship for some reason can be as counter-productive as shouting at my daughter to look happy and 'say cheese'.

But the rebellion doesn't stop there. On the way home from church I find that I just have to express my pent-up frustration that they sang that awful song again, that they shouted down the microphone again, that the computer operator couldn't keep up with the PowerPoint slides again, that the preacher ran over time again. Don't get me wrong. I love church. I love the people in my church. I also love singing and praying and preaching. At least I love them most of the time. I think.

I have it on good authority that I am not alone in having these rebellious trains of thought. I understand that many of us have similar after-service conversations on our Sunday journeys home. We analyse our 'worship' experience based on how moved we were, how bored we were, whether the music was up to spec or the preacher was on point. Even when we know better, we struggle to factor in that the only person qualified to rate our worship is the one to whom our worship is directed: God himself.

What would God say?

When I began reading the Bible through the lens of adoption, I became highly sensitised to the Bible's emphasis on care for vulnerable children. It reframed my understanding of who God is, who I am, what I was supposed to be doing with my life, how I was supposed to see my church family, and how that impacted my prayer life. In other words, it began to change the way I worshipped God, how I related to him in every part of life. But I still felt no less rebellious and critical when I went to church. Was there something wrong with me? Then I discovered something that would significantly challenge and change my view of worship.

One of the chapters in the Bible where God talks about the 'fatherless' is Isaiah 1. The book of Isaiah is full of awe-inspiring pointers to Jesus and the wonderful comfort, redemption and salvation that he would bring. It also contains the most excoriating review of corporate worship ever written, and it comes right in the first chapter. It makes those post-church-worship autopsy conversations seem quite tame. God begins by likening his people to the notorious cities of Sodom and Gomorrah, famous for their immorality and wickedness and prime examples of God's terrible judgement. If this makes for uncomfortable reading, it is only going to get worse:

> 'The multitude of your sacrifices—
>   what are they to me?' says the Lord.
> 'I have more than enough of burnt offerings,
>   of rams and the fat of fattened animals;
> I have no pleasure
>   in the blood of bulls and lambs and goats.
> When you come to appear before me,
>   who has asked this of you,
>   this trampling of my courts?
> Stop bringing meaningless offerings!
>   Your incense is detestable to me.
> New Moons, Sabbaths and convocations—
>   I cannot bear your worthless assemblies.
> Your New Moon feasts and your appointed festivals
>   I hate with all my being.
> They have become a burden to me;

I am weary of bearing them.
When you spread out your hands in prayer,
   I hide my eyes from you;
even if you offer many prayers,
   I am not listening.
Your hands are full of blood!
Wash and make yourselves clean.
   Take your evil deeds out of my sight;
   stop doing wrong.
Learn to do right . . .'

(Isaiah 1:11–17)

Why so passionate?

These verses are so brutal that it is perhaps little wonder that we hear them read out in church so infrequently. These words are not going to translate well into a praise song. No amount of drum rhythms or 'ambient worship pads' are going to be able to disguise the disgust God has for his people's corporate worship. God decries the sacrifices and festivals. Even turning up at the Temple is considered 'trampling' God's courts. And he will not even listen to their prayers. But surely this is wrong – doesn't God command us to worship him through gathering together, offering sacrifices, celebrating, praying and singing? Why does he command us here to stop and shut up?

My daughter's rebellious streak can help us. The first chapter of Isaiah says that our corporate worship can be an act of rebellion against God not because of *what* we are doing, but because of *when* we are doing it. And more importantly, this rebellion is deeply frustrating to God not because of what we *are* doing, but because of what we *are not* doing.

Isaiah is clear that what God's people have left undone is the essence of their true worship. The way we treat and defend those who are fatherless, widowed and oppressed is the worship offering God really cares about. Immediately after the passage quoted above, he reminds us to 'seek justice. Defend the oppressed. Take up the cause of the fatherless; plead the case of the widow' (Isaiah 1:17).

Understanding this vital introduction to the prophecy of Isaiah can shape the way we read the whole book, indeed the whole Bible. Grasping what God's passion really is and what lies at the heart of God's anger and behind all his warnings of judgement reframes the way we can appreciate our salvation and all the beautiful promises God offers us through Isaiah and beyond. It changes the way we appreciate worship, because it changes the way we appreciate God.

Imagine that one of my children cycles past your house each day to get to school. One morning he takes the corner too quickly and goes flying across the tarmac, skinning his arms and his legs. Luckily, he knows you live just there, and elbows his way to your door. He puts his mouth next to your conveniently located floor-level letter box and cries out for help. You recognise his voice and welcome him into your home. You bandage his wounds, you give him a hot mug of cocoa and then (with another responsible adult present so that you don't break any child-protection protocols), you put him in your car and drive him to my house. If we were acquaintances before, we are friends for life now.

But what if the scenario was slightly altered. My son comes flying off his bike near your house. He makes his way to your front door and cries for help. You recognise his voice at the letter box, but this time it reminds you of a book you are currently reading, as it happens to have been written by me. You decide it is time to thank the author. So you fire up your computer and drop me a line on social media, where in the most eloquent and articulate words possible you make known your exceeding gratitude to me. I am delighted by such an encouraging message. But later that evening, I find out that you did this instead of helping my son. You left him at the doorstep bleeding while you took the time to write to me. That encouraging message you sent me has turned into an insult. Your praise of my book only serves to remind me more forcibly of your neglect of my son in his hour of great need.

Too often it is a lot easier to substitute choruses for

caring, songs for service, piety for personal sacrifice, words for actions. This seems to be God's issue with the Israelites. They have offered God the ritual of worship but have neglected the heart of it. They have not cared for those whom God cares for. They have people on their doorsteps who are fatherless, widowed, and oppressed and in great need, but neglected them while they busied themselves with praise services and festivals, with gatherings and sacrifices. God says stop. He can't stand it any longer.

True signs of spirituality

Reading Isaiah 1 showed me that I was guilty of rebellion in my worship to God. Not because I didn't always stand and sing when I was told to by the worship leader, but because my passions and concerns didn't always match God's passions and concerns. This, I realised, was not just something God wanted me to hear from Isaiah 1. It was a theme that spilled over into the New Testament.

I noticed it in Jesus' criticisms of the ritualistic observances of the Pharisees and the teachers of the Law who tithed their herb gardens but 'neglect[ed] justice and the love of God', or who loaded people down with burdens while they themselves 'will not lift one finger to help them'.[1]

I noticed it in Jesus' life. When it came to a choice

between going to the Temple and healing a lame man,[2] he chose the latter. When it came to a choice between spending time on his own praying or attending to the needs of the crowd, again he chose the latter.[3]

I noticed it in Jesus' teaching. The parable of the sheep and the goats divides those who appeared to worship God on the basis of whether or not they fed the hungry, clothed the naked, welcomed the outcast and visited the imprisoned.[4]

I noticed it in Paul's teaching. In that masterpiece chapter on worship, 1 Corinthians 13, he notes that the outward manifestations that we might have pointed to as evidence of the Holy Spirit being present in our worship – speaking in tongues and prophecy – are nothing without the presence of the love of God. On their own they are not signs of spiritual activity but actually empty clanging carnality. Similarly, according to Paul, being able to fathom great theological and expository mysteries is nothing without love. Even sacrificial giving to the poor and facing persecution are nothing without love. Paul exhorts us to a genuine loving relationship with God that spills over into genuine practical love for our neighbour.

I noticed it in the epistle of James. He writes: 'Religion that God our Father accepts as pure and faultless is this: . . .'[5] I wonder what you would expect the punchline to be here? The term 'religion' is an unusual one in the New Testament. In the original Greek the word used here only occurs twice more, both times being used to describe veneration and worship.[6] Here, however, James is describing worship directed at God and affirming that what matters most is not that it is acceptable to us, but that it is acceptable to God. James recognises that in order for God to be able to receive our worship it needs to be 'pure and faultless', which is a phrase taken from the impeccable standards of Old Testament Temple worship.[7] Having used all the devices and language he could muster to help us frame the importance, purity and quality of worship that God is looking for, James goes on to define religion that is acceptable to God as being:

to look after orphans and widows in their distress and to keep oneself from being polluted by the world.

(James 1:27)

I have spent so much of my life as a church leader focusing my attention on the experience of the gathered worshippers, making sure that everyone in the church is happy with the volume, the style, the variety of the music, sweating over the expository clarity of the sermon and the rigour of the theology of what I was preaching. Though these things are important, it turns out that, in God's eyes, they are all irrelevant and, indeed, irreverent if they are not coupled with a concern for those in need. In James, God gives us his wish list for our worship, and at the top of it is caring for vulnerable, traumatised children.

This makes most sense when we see that at the heart of the gospel, the heart of God's mission in the universe, is our adoption and the reconciliation of all things. This makes most sense when we understand that the Spirit of adoption is the same Spirit that prompts and enables us to worship in spirit and in truth. He is the same Spirit who produces the character of Christ in us, enabling us to grow in love, joy, peace, forbearance, kindness, goodness, faithfulness, gentleness and self-control. Why? Because these are exactly the characteristics needed to care for the vulnerable and oppressed and to be united as one adopted family.

Isaiah leaves us with a challenge here. He expects us to rebel against our corporate worship. Not by being complainers or critics but by cutting through any hypocrisy in our own lives. Why aren't we doing something to stand up for the needy today? Why can't we make it part of our daily rhythm to show care for widows and orphans in whatever way we can, reflecting something of the heart God has for the vulnerable? This is the way we transform worship, the way we transcend the ritualistic habits, the way we translate God's passion into our own lives.

∼

Questions for reflection

1. What do you find yourself critiquing most in the worship gatherings of your church?

2. How does Isaiah 1 challenge the way that you view worship?

3. What are God's priorities for worship? (See James 1:27 or Matthew 25:31–46 or Isaiah 1 or 1 Corinthians 13.) What most surprises you? What may need to change in your life? What difference could this make to the Church?

Chapter 8

The secret that changes everything about justice

When it's just not fair –
and it's right under our nose.

As any parent who has more than one child will tell you, one of the most frequent complaints heard in the home is: 'It's not fair!' It's a criticism I feel keenly whenever those words are addressed to me. I love my children equally and am desperate for them to know that they have equal value, and equal access to my love and care. But when they see me giving out different amounts of pocket money, working my way through staggered bedtimes and installing or deleting different social media applications on their various mobile phone devices, often my actions are interpreted as unjust, provoking those dreaded words.

Recently that complaint was addressed to me in my local play area. Not from any of my children this time, but from another parent. We were the only two families there, and after twenty minutes the woman marched over to me, loudly complaining that my child had monopolised the swing for the entire time. Rather taken aback by her aggressive approach, as politely as I could, I muttered something about not knowing she was wanting a turn, and had she asked earlier of course I would gladly have moved my child on. Inside I was seething. I looked at her son in his private-school uniform skipping happily around the playground and stopped myself shouting back at her, 'You think that's not fair? Shall I tell you what's not fair? It's not fair that my son had no permanent family until he was four years old. It's not fair that he is so traumatised from abuse in the past that he can't enjoy most of the equipment in the play area. It's not fair that because of his hidden disabilities he finds the predict-able rocking motion of a swing soothing. It's not fair that because of government cuts he is unlikely to enjoy an education system that caters for his learning needs. It's not fair that you shouted at me for no good reason and it's not fair that I am far too well mannered to shout back at you!'

The more children I foster, the more injustices I come across. And I don't just mean the ones in my home or in my local park. There are deeply ingrained injustices in our education system, in our mental health care services, in our political system, in the biases regarding race and disabilities and religion. I have encountered injustices in social services, in passport offices, in the benefits system and even in the legal system. And the more injustices I come across, the angrier I become. I agree with my children: it's just not fair!

It's just not fair

It turns out that quite a lot of people in the Bible express their frustration that life isn't fair. Cain thought it unfair of God not to accept his offering but to accept his brother Abel's. Moses argued with God for picking him to speak to Pharaoh when his brother Aaron was the eloquent one. Jonah sulked at the injustice of God saying he was going to punish Nineveh and then having mercy on the city after all. Habakkuk complained that good things happened to bad people and bad things happened to good people. Jeremiah thought it was unfair that he was persecuted just for delivering God's message. Many of the psalmists composed laments to voice their frustrations when life just wasn't fair. I have derived great comfort from the way the Bible, by including these complaints, permits me to voice my anger towards God at the injustices I encounter.

The Bible challenges me not only to call out the injustices before God but also to speak them out in the public square. For example, we are commanded to:

Speak up for those who cannot speak for themselves,
for the rights of all who are destitute.

(Proverbs 31:8)

It is not right that children who have had the toughest starts in life are left waiting for permanent loving homes. It is not right that too many children too often 'pinball'[1] around the care system in multiple foster placements. It is not right that children with disabilities cannot access the services they need. It is not right that children caught up in war and violence have to risk their lives again by making perilous journeys trying to find refuge, only to be stranded and ignored far from home in dangerous camps. Never mind manners – I can't keep quiet about these things. After all, as I reread my Bible through the lens of adoption, I saw in Moses and the Law, and in Isaiah and the prophets, and in the Gospels and Jesus' concern for the poor, that God spoke out when things weren't fair. God spoke up for the voiceless to make sure that those who were vulnerable were protected and provided for, and he expects us to do the same.

I would never have imagined back when I adopted my daughter that it would lead to me becoming so passionate and vocal about all sorts of justice issues. But adoption, I discovered, is the secret that changes everything about justice.

Justice everywhere

I used to think justice was a dirty word. In my younger years as a Christian, many of my mentors seemed to think social justice was somehow related to the social gospel. At its worst, the social gospel movement was an attempt to spread the values of the kingdom of God on earth without necessarily recognising God as King.[2] Those who would write about and preach social restoration at the time did not seem to have much interest in spiritual renewal. And so I was taught to filter out God's care for physical needs in the Bible and see only God's interest in our spiritual needs. I became an evangelist, and at the time I understood that the extent of my responsibility was simply to pass on the good news of our salvation in terms of speaking out the message of our forgiveness, justification and redemption – an individual gospel of reconciliation with God.

Adoption changed all that for me. Our adoption into God's family does not just mean that he cares for our spiritual needs. He also cares for our social needs – welcoming us into a church family of brothers, sisters, fathers and mothers. God cares for our physical needs – he tells us that we can rely on him as our heavenly Father to provide the food for our stomachs and the clothes for our backs. God also is committed to helping us with our emotional and pastoral needs, sending the Spirit of adoption to comfort us and confirm that we have the right to call him Abba, Father. God's provision is total, you might even say holistic.

Jesus did not only speak the gospel of the kingdom with passion and clarity, he also demonstrated the kingdom of the gospel through serving the poor and standing up for the oppressed. Jesus did not have to choose between the two greatest commandments – to love God and to love our neighbour: he did both. We don't have to choose between the social gospel – caring for the needy without helping people discover a relationship with God – and the selfish gospel – offering people right standing with God without showing compassion to those around us. We are called to pass on the whole gospel, not an emaciated,[3] dualistic, edited version of the gospel, but the whole counsel of God. That means we all have some responsibility to pass on in both word and deed the good news of the availability of our full and complete salvation. Because of the Spirit of adoption, I seek to preach justification *and* practise justice; I seek to preach compassion *and* practise redemption.

The word *mišpāt* occurs in its various forms more than 200 times in the Hebrew Old Testament. Its most basic meaning is to treat people equitably. A second similar word, *tzadeqah*, refers to a life of right relationships . . . it refers to day-to-day living in which a person conducts all relationships in family and society with fairness,[4] generosity and equity. These two words are brought together scores of times in the Bible to explain the idea of justice. In a simple but telling note in the *New Dictionary of Theology*, we find that under the entry for justice it simply says 'see righteousness'.[5] Righteousness and justice in the Bible are interchangeable; they are intertwined, interconnected and indistinguishable. They are not only integral to our understanding of *who God is* as the Righteous One, the Judge of all the earth, they are also integral to our understanding of *how God acts*; he is righteous and just in all his ways. Furthermore, this is consistently shown to be *what God wants* of his people: that we seek righteousness and justice. Trying to take justice out of the Bible is like trying to take the heat out of the sun, or the university out of Oxford.

I love visiting Oxford. I have spent many hours taking my children for walks through the historic and picturesque streets, strolling through the meadows, taking photographs of the architecture, and even punting on the river. I love the multicultural feel, the connection with centuries of education, the cultural grandeur of the place. On more than one occasion I have been stopped by a tourist and asked for directions to the university. This always made me laugh in a rather bemused way. The problem is that the oldest university in the English-speaking world is not housed in a single building, nor is it even located on a campus;

its thirty-eight colleges and six permanent private halls are liberally dispersed all over the compact city. The university was literally all around those tourists as they looked for it. In it, they lived and moved and had their being. Justice is like that in the Bible. Some people can't see it there at all. But when you do see it, suddenly it is everywhere. Its architecture holds the landscape of the Bible together. Its themes fill every page. Its pursuit is woven into the very purpose of the Bible's existence. Its rhythm ripples out all around the world.

Justice for everyone

Because justice is the essence of the character of God and the heartbeat of the Bible, it is no surprise that seeking justice is also the call of every Christian. All of us who wish to walk humbly with our God should mirror God's character and obey God's command by loving mercy and acting justly. Not just as an add-on tacked on to our faith, but as an integral part of our work life, our home life and our social life, so that in it we live and move and have our being.

I have had the privilege of visiting many hundreds of churches around the world and I have been pleased to notice that it is increasingly difficult to find churches that are only concerned with meeting the needs of Christians. Most are also doing something to offer loving, practical service to their communities. Whether it is by running food banks or debt counselling services, helping elderly people or supporting refuges for abused women, providing staff to work with children and young people, resettling refugees or assisting ex-convicts to reintegrate into the community, the local church is at the forefront. The Church is waking up to the God of justice that Scripture reveals and is actively pursuing his purposes in the world.

But in many of these churches there is a disconnect between the programmes and the congregation. This works at two levels. First, fewer church members are now available to help run these events as more people work full time, so programmes are often run by paid staff. Second, those people who attend the language classes or financial support groups rarely turn up to our worship services. If they did, would we even know what to do with them? And so, for all our justice programmes, there is still the justice challenge of relational integration.

Building relational bridges between congregation and community is difficult. Many people commute to church and so have very little relational connection to the neighbourhood where the church is. Some people are busy at work and prefer to give money instead of time to help the needy – and they really don't expect to have much to do with them apart from that. Church leaders often feel the pressure of providing the kind of church experience that is expected by those who faithfully attend, and financially support, their churches. Our regular punters want excellent children's ministry, high-quality music and engaging biblical preaching, but our visiting community members may have different criteria. Some churches solve the 'problem' by running alternative services for those who come from difficult backgrounds. And still the relational gap persists.

Justice in everything

Bryan Stevenson, the American civil rights campaigner, argues that justice has to be more than something we do from a distance. When he visited black prisoners in jails in America, he began to grasp just how difficult their circumstances were, and how unjust the system was that led to one out of every three black American males spending some time in prison. Getting up from his desk in his law office and accompanying his clients into the challenging and dark places not only transformed his understanding of inequality, but also ignited his passion to change the system. He said:

> When you get proximate to the excluded and the disfavored, you learn things that you need to understand if we're going to change the world . . . Our understanding of how we change things comes in proximity to inequality, to injustice.[6]

If those we seek to help are kept at a relational arm's length, they remain projects to us rather than people. If we are happy to welcome people into church buildings and community centres but not into our homes, then we have dehumanised them. Keeping people at arm's length, at a safe distance, in detached objectivity does not accurately reflect the kind of love that God has shown us. The Spirit of adoption shows us that relational proximity changes your commitment to justice twenty-four seven.

God the Father delights in welcoming us into the same relational intimacy that he enjoys with Jesus and the Holy Spirit, and when we draw alongside others in the same way, learning their names, seeing their faces, dressing their wounds, holding them in our arms, we cannot but want to change the world for them and with them.

How many hours a week was Jesus seeking justice? How many days a month? The question is ludicrous. Jesus commanded us to be continually seeking first the kingdom of God and his righteousness–justice that that entails.[7] Justice is not just to be our hobby, or even our passion, it is to be our ontology – our way of being. Justice should be the dialect of our language, the flavour of our work assignments, the colour of our home lives, the rhythm of our footsteps.

To my surprise, adoption brought justice issues into the heart of my home. Because of the journey I have been on with my fostered and adopted children, I have fought for things I would not even have thought about before. It doesn't really matter whether a Nigerian boy has a passport or not – until he is a member of your family and you can't imagine going on holiday without him. It doesn't really matter whether the disability benefit system is fair – until you have two children with the same needs getting different amounts of support. It doesn't matter how the local government spends my income tax – until they are closing down services you know can make a world of difference to your daughter. Suddenly I am reading policy documents and writing campaign letters late at night and collaring my MP and signing petitions. Suddenly it doesn't matter whether my politics are red, blue, green or gold – or whether the budget will make me better or worse off. Those children in my home who are already massively disadvantaged need someone to fight for them, and as the dad in their lives, I will be their champion whatever it takes.

Jesus knew that parenting changes us, and that it can offer powerful insights into our relationship with God the Father. He said:

> *Which of you, if your son asks for bread, will give him a stone? Or if he asks for a fish, will give him a snake? If you, then, though you are evil, know how to give good gifts to your children, how much more will your Father in heaven give good gifts to those who ask him! So in*

everything, do to others what you would have them do
to you, for this sums up the Law and the Prophets.

(Matthew 7:9–12)

Whatever I do for my children pales into insignificance compared with God's great and generous love and provision for us. I can bask in that wonderful promise for a long time. But that was never meant to be the end of the story. It's not an excuse to sit back, it's a motivation to step forward. The Law and the prophets are full of stories and injunctions and commands to treat people generously and fairly. Jesus notes this and raises the bar, as he does throughout the Sermon on the Mount. He says that the way we have experienced God's father–child provision and advocacy is the model for the way we are to champion justice for others. The Spirit of adoption changes everything about justice. And justice can be as close as our kitchen table.

～

Questions for reflection

1. Why do you think Christians often divide up the good news of the gospel and the good deeds of the gospel? How does remembering our adoption into God's family help to keep these things together?

2. How do we avoid our involvement with justice being

limited to tokenism, hobbies, fads, programmes or
rotas? What would it take to stop seeing justice as
an add-on, and to begin to bring justice into the
heart of everything we are and do?

3. What practical steps can you make today to speak
about and demonstrate our heavenly Father's love
for the world?

Chapter 9

The secret that changes everything about suffering

When we can't resolve the problems –
and we can embrace the suffering.

I don't like suffering. I'm bad enough when I've got a cold or the flu. I feel so sorry for myself sometimes I curl up and plan my own funeral. Take your vitamins, my mum used to say. Keep fit and healthy. Look after number one. Don't mix with the wrong crowd. Walk away from trouble, she told me. And so I tried to steer well clear of suffering at all costs, just like she said. Then I became a Christian. That's when I discovered that Jesus was not like my mum. Instead of avoiding suffering, Christians, it appears, are supposed to search it out.

Blessed are you when people insult you, persecute you and falsely say all kinds of evil against you because of me. Rejoice and be glad, because great is your reward in heaven, for in the same way they persecuted the prophets who were before you.

(Matthew 5:11–12)

But before all this, they will seize you and persecute you. They will hand you over to synagogues and put you in prison, and you will be brought before kings and governors, and all on account of my name. And so you will bear testimony to me.

(Luke 21:12–13)

Remember what I told you: 'A servant is not greater than his master.' If they persecuted me, they will persecute you also.

(John 15:20)

For it has been granted to you on behalf of Christ not only to believe in him, but also to suffer for him.

(Philippians 1:29)

But rejoice inasmuch as you participate in the sufferings of Christ, so that you may be overjoyed when his glory is revealed.

(1 Peter 4:13)

The promise of suffering

It has to be said that none of these verses were pointed out to me before I became a Christian. It is one of those cover-ups that most of us discover after conversion. Like the small print on the contract of a mobile phone, you only really read the true ongoing costs for that incredible bargain that seemed too good to be true when something goes wrong with your device. The suffering clause is not advertised as one of Christianity's key features, but as soon as trouble hits, you are also hit with the hard truth that this was always part of the deal.

Jesus, Peter and Paul did not shy away from being honest and upfront about suffering for the sake of Christ being part and parcel of the normal Christian calling. Moreover, they specifically highlighted the part we often prefer to leave in the small print, by explaining suffering in terms of a promise, a privilege and even a pleasure! What was their secret for having such a transformed perspective on suffering? Can the Spirit of adoption help us in any way to dovetail our own attitudes with that of the Bible?

The paradox of suffering

Ironically, it was my own aversion to suffering that motivated me to begin my adoption journey. Living and travelling in Eastern Europe in the 1980s and 90s, my wife and I came across many of the orphanages where children were caged up like animals, shaved like criminals and quarantined from human interaction like viruses. When the media began highlighting these terrible practices, one of the consequences was that more children appeared on the streets. Everywhere we went we saw the terrible need, but could do nothing, as any attempts to help were seen as further judgement and interference. When we returned to the UK, we saw that we could alleviate something of the global suffering of children separated from their families by using the 'starfish' principle. This idea stems from the oft-told story of the boy walking along a beach who comes across a thousand dying starfish left stranded by the tide. He has just thrown one back in the sea when an old man passes by and asks him why he bothers – he can't make a difference to such a massive problem. The boy astutely replies that it had made a difference to that one, now safely back in the sea. Faced with the huge global crisis of children growing up without families, perhaps we could make a difference for that one, out of many millions in need, growing up in our home.

When we adopted our daughter, we realised that although we had set out to alleviate suffering, something more profound had happened. The traumatic family background from which she had come, the cycle of neglect and abuse that had caused chaos through generations, was not a story that had now been resolved by us

– rather, it was a story that now involved us. It was still part of *her* story and it had now become part of *our* story. We had somehow become united with her in the suffering.

This shed new light on Paul's teaching about our spiritual adoption:

> *the Spirit you received brought about your adoption to sonship . . . Now if we are children, then we are heirs – heirs of God and co-heirs with Christ, if indeed we share in his sufferings in order that we may also share in his glory.*
>
> *(Romans 8:15, 17)*

When Jesus set out on his mission to save his people for adoption into his family, he saw our suffering and became part of it. He suffered in every way, was tempted and was tortured physically, emotionally, socially and spiritually. He shared our darkest paths. Our story became his story. And when Jesus suffered and died on the cross to redeem us and justify us and adopt us, he called us to share in his sufferings too. He told us to take up our cross and follow him. His story became our story.

Dietrich Bonhoeffer recognised that the cross unites us with Christ not only through the once-for-all sacrifice made, but also through the ongoing suffering shared:

> *The cross is laid on every Christian. As we embark upon discipleship we surrender ourselves to Christ in union*

with his death – we give over our lives to death. Thus
it begins; the cross is not the terrible end to an otherwise
god-fearing and happy life, but it meets us at the begin-
ning of our communion with Christ. When Christ calls
a man, he bids him come and die.[1]

The circumstances that led to my daughter being
adopted were in one sense a terrible ending, and in
another sense a wonderful beginning. The cross plays
this pivotal role in our lives as Christians. Suffering
marks the birth of our adoption story, and it also marks
the path of our adoption journey. There is a paradox
here. God, our heavenly Father, who has paid the great
cost, who is committed to our well-being, who promises to meet every need we have, also provides us with
a lifetime of hardship. Can you imagine what a social
worker would do if I welcomed a child into my care
by offering to carry their burdens, and then promising
to weigh them down with a few burdens of mine in
return? I would fail the assessment forthwith. How
can it be okay for God to promise us suffering when
he also promised to protect us, have compassion on
us, never forget us and graciously give us all things?
What kind of father would do that?

This paradox is one that the book of Job wrestles
with, and it is worth exploring because there is a
surprising connection here between suffering and
adoption that can help us.

The purpose of suffering

I have always been challenged by the story of Job because here is someone who experiences the most unbearable and extreme suffering and yet still remains faithful to God. I have also been troubled by the story of Job because the Bible makes it very clear that the terrible things that happen to him are not a series of unfortunate events but an orchestration of extreme suffering that is specifically permissioned by God himself.

The narrative[2] introduces a man of unblemished character who was revered in the region. Then it peels back a layer to reveal what effect Job's life and character has in the heavenly realm. What we find is a form of divine courtroom where Satan is some kind of (un-)angelic prosecutor, laying down his challenge to God. Satan argues that Job's devotion to God is based purely on the fact that life has been good to him, and if all of the blessings were stripped away, he, like anyone else, would surely renounce his love for God. In response to this challenge a deal is struck: God agrees that Job will be a test case. Despite the blatant challenge to his authority and the attack on his character, God permits Satan to bring suffering into Job's life. The essential question that runs through the rest of the book is whether Job will still honour God when all of his prosperity is taken from him, or whether he will 'curse [God] to [his] face'.[3]

Sometimes it seems that our loving heavenly Father may allow us to suffer because there are other factors in play that we cannot see or understand from where we are. God is willing to let Job suffer because of a wider cosmic conflict that needed to be resolved. We see this again in the suffering of Jesus. God the Father loves his Son, but for the sake of the salvation of humanity and the restoration of all things, God allows Jesus to suffer. When I see the terrible suffering around me and it feels like such a waste, I cannot imagine how God could either orchestrate it for a greater good or even weave it into something vaguely okay. Nevertheless, the sufferings of Job and Jesus give me a glimmer of hope that suffering may lead to more positive outcomes than it may appear to.

I hope that my daughter will one day understand something of the redemptive logic of suffering. When she was adopted into our family, one thing that happened immediately was that she changed from being a fostered child to being a fostering child in a fostering family. This has resulted in her being exposed to some of the terrible stories and distresses of those children that have come through our family from the care system, some with backgrounds similar to her own. She has made sacrifices without question over the years, and the care and compassion she has shown her foster siblings has helped them to experience love and mercy.

Watching her and my other children suffer for the sake of others in the home has sometimes made my heart ache in pain for them, and sometimes made it swell with pride in them. Sometimes watching them suffer for the sake of others has made me want to quit being a foster carer. They would have had so much more space and attention and freedom without foster children around, and I long to give them those things in abundance. But suffering does not always make you resentful, as Job shows us. Watching my children grow in kindness and empathy and generosity not just despite their sacrifices, but because of them has helped me understand something of God's promise to work all things for good for the sake of those who love him.

When someone tells me that they have adopted a child, it fills me with joy and admiration. I congratulate them profusely, and love to share with them the incredible privileges of being an adoptive father. But I know also that for that adoption to have taken place there must have been extreme suffering. Separation from their birth family is no small thing, no matter what age the child is at the time. Any history of neglect, abuse, violence, poverty and displacement leaves psychological scars on even the tiniest of babies. And the suffering of the child is only part of the bigger story. Behind every child in care is a grieving, sick or damaged parent. Sometimes two. Often grandparents and siblings and aunts and uncles are affected too as they watch their family torn apart. Then the suffering is taken on not only by adoptive parents, but by adoptive grandparents, aunts, uncles and siblings.

Adoptive mum, author and youth activist Rachel Gardner put it like this:

> *Sometimes we feel overwhelmed by the fact that our two children, born to other people, call us 'Mumma' and 'Dada'. It carries with it feelings of unspeakable joy and deep sadness at the same time. Even as we seek to be the parents to our children God calls us to be, it breaks our hearts that there are birth families out there who don't get to be with the children they brought into the world. I know we're not the only ones who know what it is to hold the joy and the sorrow in tension.*[4]

There is no adoption without suffering. They usually arrive hand in hand. They usually go through life hand in hand. Adoption cannot simply be seen as a rags-to-riches story. The rags and riches weave together. There is dust and there are sparkles of diamond. Beauty and ashes, joy and sorrow. If, as the Bible says, adoption is the ultimate purpose of the universe, then suffering must have a purpose too. Even Job's unhelpful friends knew that. They were just looking for it in the wrong place.

The power of suffering

There have always been narrow-minded, theologically naive and downright unhelpful believers far too willing to force their opinions on others in their times of weakness. Job's counsellors prove themselves to be ignorant, not only of their God, but of their friend too. They present Job with a litany of accusations that make him look back and check not only his actions but his motives too. In his reflection, he offers a most remarkable picture of his life:

> *If I have denied justice to any of my servants,*
> *whether male or female,*
> *when they had a grievance against me,*
> *what will I do when God confronts me?*
> *What will I answer when called to account?*
> *Did not he who made me in the womb make them?*
> *Did not the same one form us both within our*
> *mothers?*
> *If I have denied the desires of the poor*
> *or let the eyes of the widow grow weary,*
> *If I have kept my bread to myself,*
> *not sharing it with the fatherless—*
> *but from my youth I reared them as a father would,*
> *and from my birth I guided the widow—*
> *if I have seen anyone perishing for lack of clothing,*
> *or the needy without garments,*

and their hearts did not bless me
    for warming them with the fleece from my sheep,
if I have raised my hand against the fatherless,
    knowing that I had influence in court,
then let my arm fall from the shoulder,
    let it be broken off at the joint.
For I dreaded destruction from God,
    and for fear of his splendour I could not do such
    things.

(Job 31:13–23)

Job presents here a radical understanding of human life. In cultures where people would have assumed that wealth and heritage made some people more important or more valuable than others, he presents an understanding of human value and dignity that shines with the noblest aspects of politics, equality and human rights, thousands of years before such ideas were normalised in theory at least. His motivation was his righteous respect for our common creator, and his godly fear of our common judge. Because we all share the same origin story and we all have to give an account of ourselves before God, Job believed that everyone should be treated with equity and righteousness.

This was not just doctrine for Job. This was worked out in the way he cared for the needy and vulnerable and, particularly, the fatherless. His description reminds me of the work of foster carers and adopters with vulnerable children. He mentions the practical assistance of providing food and clothing. He mentions the emotional proximity that comes with child-rearing and offering guidance. He mentions the relational privileges of blessing and being blessed. And he mentions the professional advocacy of using his power and influence for the sake of the fatherless, actively seeking their welfare, not only avoiding doing them harm. When he speaks of 'raising a hand against the fatherless', he may be referring to a miscarriage of justice, a dodgy business deal or physical abuse:[5] Job claims innocence on all three counts, citing his ultimate respect for the glory and judgement of God.

When others suffered, Job reached out to them and stood up for them. And when Job himself suffered, those selfless actions enabled him to face down his critics and maintain perspective. At this stage in the book Job's suffering has been going on a while, and yet he can still claim to be innocent of ignoring or exploiting the needy. Even in the middle of his own suffering Job continued to care for those around him in need. This seems to suggest that the power of suffering to shake or disrupt our faith may be offset to some degree by our power in alleviating the suffering of others.

This is not to say that caring for the vulnerable insulates you from difficulties. Job continues to suffer terribly, even though he is just and righteous and committed to the welfare of the needy. I meet many people who make incredible sacrifices for the sake of others, and yet also face incredible challenges of their own. Sometimes we receive suffering not only *as* we relieve suffering in others, but *because* we relieve suffering in others. Job, in his own wrestling with the cause-and-effect questions of his suffering, at least had one thing to hold on to: his understanding of who God is compelled him to help others in need, and the more involved he got, the more he understood God. His sufferings were terribly hard, but he would endure them. His faith would be shaken, but it would also be strengthened.

The pursuit of suffering

Christians are as likely to face suffering as firefighters are to face burning buildings and lifeboat volunteers to face rough seas. A doctor running away at the sight of blood, a zookeeper who can't stand being around snakes, and a pilot terrified of flying would have major problems in their chosen vocations. A Christian who isn't willing to endure suffering is in the same category. As Paul writes, 'everyone who wants to live a godly life in Christ Jesus will be persecuted'.[6]

In the previous verses, Paul had referred to some of his persecutions and sufferings, and said that they had not detracted from his teaching, way of life, purpose, faith, patience, love and endurance. I cannot read these lines without thinking of stories I have heard of Christians around the world in extreme situations. I think of Perpetua, a young woman in Roman times who refused to renounce her love for Christ even though she knew it would cost her her life and she would not be able to bring up the baby she had just given birth to. I think of Christians in Burundi and Rwanda who, because they refused to participate in racial discrimination practices, were butchered by machetes. I have met Christians from Syria, from the former Soviet Union, from North Korea, whose terrible sufferings make any difficulties I have faced seem relatively insignificant. Their endurance, like Job's, deeply challenges me when I am tempted to say that life is hard or when I feel unwilling to make sacrifices for the sake of others.

Job embraced those who were suffering around him, and pursued justice for them, because he understood God's heart for those who suffer. This legacy, particularly in regard to caring for the fatherless,[7] helped him when he found himself in the middle of troubles of his own, with his own family stripped from him. It did not take away the pain and the questions and the struggles, as the forty chapters of the book attest, but it did help him to trust God when things happened that he could not understand and when people accused him of things that were not true. It enabled him to persevere to the end and not lose his faith.

When I found myself struggling in a pointless and hopeless situation, it happened to coincide with my discovery of the biblical thread of caring for the fatherless. I could relate to Job a little in my care for my adopted child. My colleagues – sometimes my accusers, sometimes my comforters – made me question my life, my ministry and my motives. Unlike Job, I found a lot of faults and failings that I had to hold my hand up to. However, also unlike Job, I had the whole of the Bible to help me. I understood much more of the spiritual battle than he could see. I understood much more of the spiritual victory than he could know. I read Jesus' promise not to leave us as orphans,[8] but to give us the Holy Spirit. I began to learn that because of the Spirit of adoption, there is an antidote to fear, to hopelessness, to self-destructive thoughts. In suffering there is comfort, there is a Father to whom we can cry, there is a future, there is hope, there is glory.

Dr Tim Keller, in his reflection on Romans 8, puts it like this:

Our adoption means we are loved like Christ is loved. We are honoured like he is honoured – every one of us – no matter what. Your circumstances cannot hinder or threaten that promise. In fact, your bad circumstances will only help you understand and even claim the beauty of that promise. The more you live out who you are in

Christ, the more you become like him in actuality. Paul is not promising you better life circumstances; he is promising you a far better life. He's promising you a life of greatness. He is promising you a life of joy. He's promising you a life of humility. He's promising you a life of nobility. He's promising you a life that goes on forever.[9]

~

Questions for reflection

1. What are the ways you have had to suffer as a Christian? To what extent did you see your difficulties as sharing in Christ's suffering?
2. Think of all the ways that adoption and suffering go hand in hand. How could this give us hope, endurance, purpose and comfort?
3. Read again Job's defence in chapter 31 quoted above. How does the 'fear of [God's] splendour' compel you to live differently from those around you?

Chapter 10

The secret that changes everything about holiness

Conforming to the family likeness –
and daring to be different.

She is tall, I am short. She has big, beautiful, curly blonde hair. I have a diminishing amount of black hair. She has ancestry from one side of the globe, and I, well, it's complicated, but basically mine is from the opposite side of the globe. My adopted daughter has no biological connection with my ancestry. And yet strangers often remark how alike we are. It happened so often it got me wondering. What on earth were people seeing? I asked around a bit and this is what people told me. We both have eyes that sparkle. We both smile a lot. We are both energetic and bubbly. We both talk constantly. We love being out and about and meeting people. We remember faces. We love music. We relish joking around and winding up other members of the family. We can both eat crisps until they are coming out of our ears. The list went on. It turns out that even though there is little similarity physically, people nevertheless see a similarity because of behaviour and personality. Nurture has trumped nature.

This little insight helped me a lot when it came to understanding holiness – first, because becoming like God and like Jesus may be a slow-developing process of relational osmosis, however differently you start out. Second, because sometimes others can see this more in you than you can notice yourself. And third, because when adoption is involved the shared traits of family likeness can be both more surprising and more significant than we might imagine.

It was time to take a closer look at the Bible to see if viewing it through this lens of adoption could help me understand holiness better.

Be conformed

My starting point was the extraordinarily challenging verse in 1 Peter:

> *As obedient children, do not conform to the evil desires you had when you lived in ignorance. But just as he who called you is holy, so be holy in all you do; for it is written: 'Be holy, because I am holy.'*
>
> *(1 Peter 1:14–16)*

Peter clearly notes our status as God's children, and the link between nature and nurture, being and behaving. We are to *be* holy, and to *do* holy. Holiness is to mark who we are *and* what we do. But how does that work out in practice? What does it look like? My youth group leader always talked about holiness as things we did *not* do: excessive drinking, taking drugs, shoplifting, rock music, tattoos. It was sometimes hard to work out which of these were sins in the eyes of God and which were sins in the eyes of the youth leader. Peter, too, at first sight seems to present holiness in this negative way, telling us not to conform to the evil desires. It took me a while to understand this in the wider context of Peter's letter, where he describes other positive family traits that come from being like Jesus.

Peter's idea of holiness as a process of conforming brought me back to Romans 8, that great chapter that centres on the Spirit of adoption. Later in the chapter Paul writes this:

> *And we know that in all things God works for the good of those who love him, who have been called according to his purpose. For those God foreknew he also predestined to be conformed to the image of his Son, that he might be the firstborn among many brothers and sisters. And those he predestined, he also called; those he called, he also justified; those he justified, he also glorified.*
>
> *(Romans 8:28–30)*

God has a purpose for our lives. In all things, even in the mess and chaos, even with the abuse and violence and suffering we see around us, God is working something good out. This is not to say God is the author of evil (even in the book of Job, God does not directly cause the suffering to Job, but allows Satan some degree of influence over him). Rather, God can take the bad in our lives and in the world and somehow redemptively weave them into something good. Like a tattoo fixer who can design a new intricately designed tattoo using the lines of a bad one, God can turn ugly into beautiful, shameful into admirable, mistakes into masterpieces. In fact, the creativity and ingenuity of a tattoo fixer is best demonstrated by the more disastrous tattoos they have to try and rework. In the same way, when God makes all things work together for good, he takes the broken pieces of our lives, the tragedies of our story, the disasters of our history, and creates them into something more wonderful and incredible than we could imagine.

It is God's work to make us beautiful, good and holy. It is his purpose not just to brush us up a little, but to conform us to the image or likeness of Jesus. The Greek word for likeness, *eikon*, is the root of our word 'icon'. These days the word 'icon' usually conjures up in our minds the little images used to represent apps and computer programs. One click on the icon and the full program is launched. But this is a great illustration of our role in the world. We are to be God's icons,[1] representing him in the world so that people can look at us and see the likeness, the link to God himself. Jesus is the perfect icon of God in this respect. Not only that, Jesus is the perfect icon for us as the eldest brother among many sisters and brothers. Paul here is reminding us of the picture of adoption he painted earlier. The purpose of God from creation to new creation[2] is the formation of a new family through adoption. And now we find out that this new family is to resemble the Son of God, and that God is doing this holiness work in us.

One little boy who came into our family at the age of seven was physically stronger than me. He had been known to throw chairs through double-glazed windows. The teachers at school could not restrain him when he had a meltdown, even two or three staff together. We were not told this when we were asked to take him in, but we soon learned just how strong he was. The slightest anxiety would cause him to run into roads, slam his fist into walls and lash out at those who were trying to protect him. How was this placement ever going to work? How could he fit into family life when he was a danger to himself and others? It was no good telling him to behave, to conform, to change his ways. The damage that others had caused him over the years had created such an extreme fight-or-flight mentality that his panicked reactions had become ingrained. It was not his responsibility to manage that at the age of seven. It was mine. Because he was part of my family, I had to provide him, as best I could, with a calm environment, a predictable environment, a fun environment, a loving, safe home with clear and consistent boundaries and lots of lovely things to look forward to. My eldest sons became role-model foster brothers for him, channelling energy into sports and aggression into an Xbox controller. Gradually the triggers subsided and the reactions became less extreme. A transformation began.

What a powerful picture that is of God's work in us. We were out of control, damaged by the sinful environment that we grew up in. God knew we could not change by ourselves. So he stepped in to adopt us, to bring us home, to give us positive relationships, different expectations, a perfect role model. Gradually, because of God's work in our lives, we are conformed to the image of our elder brother, Jesus. There will be a family likeness. There will be transformation.

Be different

I once knew a boy who was adopted into a family that already had a child the same age as him. Before long, I noticed that the parents started dressing the adopted child like his brother, giving him the same haircut, the same school bags. Was this their way of treating them equally? Or was this their way of making sure he conformed to their idea of a son? I feared that his uniqueness was being squeezed out by controlling parents who had an idealised picture in their head of who their adopted son should be. Sometimes, when it comes to holiness, I worry that God may be like that too. Does he have an unrealistic picture of who we should be? Does he not accept us the way we are? Is he forcing me into a mould that I don't fit? Are we always going to be compared with the perfect older brother and be found wanting?

To find the answer to this, we need to work out what it means to be conformed to the image of Jesus. Jesus has many incredible attributes to which we are to aspire. He is compassionate, faithful, just, righteous, loving, gentle, strong, courageous and much, much more. He also has some attributes that we can never achieve. In the verses from Romans above, Paul makes this distinction by calling him the 'firstborn'. Of course he was not literally born – he is the eternal son of God. He is 'firstborn' in the sense that he has priority over us. He is the Word of God incarnate. He is the resurrected King before whom every knee will bow. He is omnipotent, omniscient, omnipresent. Because of our adoption we are somehow given the same intimacy and welcome that Jesus has to God the Father. But we are not, and never will be, the same as Jesus.

I have enjoyed watching the Netflix series *The Crown* as it tries to reconstruct what might have happened behind the closed doors of Buckingham Palace during the reign of Queen Elizabeth II. Sometimes it feels almost sacrilegious to wonder how the Queen fell in love and what it was like for her struggling to handle the pressure of national and familial crises. But, for me, one of the most interesting relationships is the one between the Queen and her sister, Princess Margaret. The two sisters are the same in so many ways, and yet one became queen and sovereign, while the other remained a princess and a subject, which brings all sorts of complications into their relationship. In a royal family your sister can be your queen; in the same way, in our spiritual family, as the adopted children of the King of the Universe, our older brother is also our Lord.

When we are adopted into God's family we can recognise that there are unique things about Jesus but there are also unique things about us, too. God has made each of us distinct and special, and at the end of time, he pictures beauty in the diversity that he sees. In the book of Revelation, we are told that all the nations will gather to sing praise to Jesus, as a great crowd made up of people from every tribe and language.[3] So even though we are conformed to the likeness of the Son, God relates to us individually; he gives us different gifts, skills, experiences, personalities, so that as a rich, diverse family we together reflect the wonders of the grace and glory of God. There is a family likeness, yet we are all still very different.

To be able to understand holiness we need to grasp both our common goal and our unique call. Yes, we are being conformed to the likeness of Jesus. But we will still be different from each other. And we are certainly different from the world. My daughter may resemble me, she may reflect something of me, but she is not me. I want my daughter to blend into my family well, to know she is one of us, but I also want her (just as I do my other children) to stand out, to find her niche, make her mark and be extraordinary. At school, while her friends and her teachers are often preaching conformation, I am daring her to be different. Different from the world. And different for God.

Be distinct

I remember waiting on the red carpet, loitering with intent. I had somehow managed to blag tickets for the world premiere of a film in London's Leicester Square. I had borrowed a tuxedo from a teenage member of our church and was as smart as I could make myself. We were supposed to go into the cinema ahead of the major celebrities and then patiently watch their arrival on the big screen. I had other plans. I wanted to meet the stars, to shake hands with the director. And because it was a royal premiere, perhaps catch a glimpse of the Queen herself, wearing 3D glasses for the first time. But the longer I waited and loitered, the more the security men with their dark glasses and earpieces made sure I kept well back. They were on a mission to make sure people like me didn't get near Her Majesty. And so I gave up. I obviously wasn't special enough, smart enough, famous enough to be anywhere near the Queen.

Some of us are like this when it comes to holiness. It seems like we have tickets to access God, but we end up just waiting around, too far away to get a close look, until eventually we give up even trying to enjoy being in the presence of our King. God is too difficult to access. He is holy. And we are not. Nothing we can do will ever bridge the immense gap between us.

The Old Testament reinforces this idea of separation. The Temple system separates off the Holy of Holies. It is strictly off limits except to a small number of very special people under very special ceremonial circumstances. And then God gave laws to help his people distinguish between the clean and the unclean, the holy and the common. Even the days of the week were separated, so that one day was set apart to be 'holy'.[4] But the New Testament seems to present a new way. The curtain around the Holy of Holies is ripped in two. Jesus walks around with no red carpet in sight. He spends his time with the lowest of the low. He blesses the children that nobody else wanted him to see, he heals the sick who had no hope even on the seventh day of the week, he hangs out with the sinners and tax collectors. It was no wonder the religious elites were outraged. If Jesus were the Messiah, God's holy servant, the undefiled High Priest, then why would he allow himself to be tainted by being in the presence of the undeserving? It was a scandal.[5] What Jesus surely needed was some security men with dark glasses and earpieces to keep the riff-raff away.

The Bible presents us with this conundrum regarding holiness. On the one hand, holiness demands separation. But on the other hand, holiness also demands hospitality. The Pharisees could not resolve the paradox. Even today Christians tend to polarise towards one camp or the other. But true holiness is embracing both tenets. It is hating the sin and loving the sinner. It is truth and grace. It is a pure heart and an open spirit. For Jesus, holiness was never compromised. He did not distance himself, but drew near. He embraced the prodigals and forgave the profligate, offered grace to the prostitutes and touched the lepers. He lived a perfect life and then he died the perfect death so that the stain of sin could be removed and we could freely access the Holy of Holies.

Unfortunately, many of us compromise holiness on both counts. Instead of hating the sin in our lives, we choose just to dislike it, to avoid it if we have to, to excuse it when we can, to learn to live with it. And instead of loving the sinner, we prefer to socialise with the acceptable, the religious, the fit and healthy.

The Spirit of adoption challenges us. God chose us to be welcomed into his family even when we were unacceptable, sacrilegious, sick, broken. We who were far away have been brought near.[6] We who were unclean and contaminated have not just been cleansed, we have been welcomed into the family of God, redeemed, restored, forgiven, purified and adopted. We have received radical hospitality from the most holy God who is committed to conforming us to the likeness of Christ, and to celebrating our uniqueness and diversity. Now that we are different, distinct and set apart for God's purposes, will we mirror that Spirit of adoption in our lives, compelled by the Holy Spirit to seek out the needy, the lost, the sinful, the broken and the displaced? Just like Jesus did.

But isn't that dangerous? Won't that just bring trouble and hardship into our lives? Won't we be accused of compromising our faith? Won't that cause us to suffer and tempt us to sin? Won't we wind up losing our access to God? The rest of Romans 8 addresses these questions. The answers are yes, yes, yes, yes, and definitively no. Paul concludes:

For I am convinced that neither death nor life, neither angels nor demons, neither the present nor the future, nor any powers, neither height nor depth, nor anything else in all creation, will be able to separate us from the love of God that is in Christ Jesus our Lord.

(Romans 8:38–9)

When I adopted my daughter I asked the social worker questions. Can this be undone? Could a birth relative turn up and claim rights over her? Is there a legal loophole that I need to be aware of? What if my circumstances changed? What if I moved to a different country? I was told definitively no, an adoption order cannot be revoked. Nothing can separate us legally as father and daughter. It is an irreversible decision. For those of us worried that our connection to God seems flimsy and fragile or temporary and insecure, that our faith wavers with our circumstances, that it fades with distance, or that it will fail under pressure, God wants us to know that our adoption is absolute. God calls us to be separate from the world, but the world cannot separate us from his love. He calls us to be the best we can be, while accepting us just the way we are. He is conforming us to the likeness of Jesus, and is conferring on us equal rights, even though we would never be holy and blameless without his grace. We cannot separate holiness from hospitality when it comes to the way God has accepted and adopted us. Perhaps holiness and hospitality should always go together in our lives too.

Questions for reflection

1. In what ways do you resemble your earthly family? In what ways do you resemble your heavenly family?
2. Reflect on the theme of separation in the Bible. You can find it in Genesis 1, Leviticus 20:22–6, Isaiah 59, Matthew 25, Romans 8. How does this theme point towards the holiness of God?
3. Why was Jesus criticised for his hospitality? How can our hospitality demonstrate the holiness of God?

Epilogue

A letter

To my dear daughter,

I remember the moment you first arrived. A tiny, beautiful, sleepy newborn baby placed in my arms, while your brothers and sister danced around the room, pausing only occasionally to creep close and gaze into your eyes. I laid you in the Moses basket, remembering that Moses was the first fostered child and first adopted child in the Bible and, with God's help, went on to change the world. I knew you were our first fostered child, but I did not know then that you would be our first adopted child too. I knew I had changed your world, but I did not know then that you would change my world too.

There were lots of things I did not know. I did not know your future. I did not know your history. But I did know that the nine months of assessments, of waiting, had all been worth it. There was mystery, and there was you, real and helpless, tiny and momentous. I was in no doubt that you were absolutely precious, perfectly unique and already deeply treasured. I wondered how it was possible to feel so fiercely protective over someone with no biological connection to myself, someone I had only just met. Well, you brought joy and wonder into our family from the moment you arrived, and you still do today.

As your little personality grew and developed and got stronger despite the legal wrestling in the background, I faced problems of my own. They were such heavy burdens, I thought I might collapse under the weight of them. Your smile, and the way your brothers and sisters elicited it, kept me going hour by hour. And when the moment came that we finally legally adopted you, I realised things would never be the same again. The celebration at the ice-cream parlour gave me a taste of what heaven will be like – the joy of becoming a forever family after so many obstacles and difficulties.

I had thought that by adopting you I was rescuing you, providing you with a home and a hope for the future, passing on to you all the wisdom I had gleaned in life. But it wasn't long before I realised that you were teaching me, helping me, showing me more profound truths than I had learned in any Bible college. In the midst of chaos and despair, there can be hope. Despite trouble and hardship, there can be resilience. If I could care for you so deeply and fight for you so determinedly, then God, whose love is infinite, must feel even more passionately about you – and about me. He is our Father.

It has been one of my life's ambitions to be the best dad I can be to you. I want my fatherhood to point you to your heavenly Father. I know I get it wrong a lot. I often miscommunicate, misunderstand, and I make many mistakes. Maybe this, too, points to God – you and I together need a Father who is perfect in all of his ways. He is there when I fail. He can turn all things to good.

You make mistakes sometimes too. You get frustrated and angry with yourself, and with me. You dislike yourself occasionally and think you don't deserve my love, or God's. It breaks my heart – not because I am disappointed in you, but because I am desperate for you to know that, in God's eyes and in mine, you are perfect. You have been fearfully and wonderfully made and God doesn't make mistakes. When things go wrong, my love for you doesn't stop. Even my discipline is an expression of my protective love for you. I'm not trying to make you the same as your brothers and sisters, I am trying to help you become the unique you God made you to be.

One of my biggest fears is that you will misinterpret my love. That when I am angry with something you have done, you may imagine I am angry with you. That you might see my hopes for you as expectations, my care for you as duty, my discipline of you as dissatisfaction with you. I imagine that you might imagine that I stole you from your birth family, adopted you for my own ends, and that now I resent being stuck with you. Nothing is further from the truth. Whatever you feel, I can assure you my love for you is real, unconditional and everlasting. Not perfect, but as close as I can get.

There is a story in the Bible that plays on my fears. It's one I have told you many times. It's about a father whose son walks away from the family. He turns his back on the ones who have cared for him his whole life, with no intention of ever seeing them again. He thinks he would be better off without them, and gets as far away as he can go. Jesus said that that father was like God. If a child can walk away from a perfect father, then I sometimes wonder what hope *I* have – what right do I have to hold on to you?

I have never met a teenager who doesn't go through questions about their identity. I have never met a teenager who doesn't struggle a bit with their relationship with their parents. It is natural for young adults to dream about leaving home. But for adopted children, sometimes those years can have an extra dimension of complexity. Perhaps they think the grass could be greener somewhere else. Perhaps they believe the films that romanticise a renewed acquaintance with the birth family. One day you will leave home, and I hope it will be something we plan together and enjoy together. I really hope so. It could be a lot of fun. You have so much to offer the world, and I would love to be a part of it. But maybe it won't happen quite like that.

The boy in the story takes his share of the inheritance prematurely and leaves home on his own terms, breaking the heart of his father. Because he has money to spend, he also has lots of friends and, for a while, life is good. But when the money runs out, his friends run out too. He tries to get work, but the only job he can get is the one nobody else wants to stoop to. He is in a bad place. That's when he realises that home, for all its frustrations, was not so bad after all. He rehearses an apology and heads back to ask for a lifeline – it's his only hope.

You know what happens next. The story zooms in to the father, waiting and waiting for his child to come back. Everyone tells him not to bother. The child wouldn't dare come back. He is probably dead. But the father waits anyway. And one day he sees someone coming down the road towards him. It looks remarkably like the boy he last saw walking in the opposite direction. The pace is slower, the mood is more solemn, but he would recognise that gait anywhere – he was the one who had taught the boy to walk in the first place. And just like that time when, as a baby, his son had taken his first steps, the father opens out his arms in encouragement and welcome and embrace. It is a momentous occasion.

In that embrace is one of the most amazing pictures of God's love for us. The lad is filthy, covered in dust, mud and unmentionably worse, but the father embraces him anyway. The lad says something about not deserving anything – and he doesn't – but the father embraces him anyway. The boy doesn't even have to mention the obvious thing – that all the money is gone – the father continues to embrace him anyway. The neighbours laugh at the indignity, and the older brother is indignant, but the father embraces the boy anyway. He gives him new clothes and prepares a celebration feast. His son, who had, by claiming his inheritance prematurely, permanently and officially removed himself from the family, is now, as signalled by the ring on his finger, officially adopted back into the family, fully reinstated as a son.

I love this story. You might think that I, as your dad, relate mainly to the adopting father. But to be honest, I relate more closely to the adopted child. I spent many years turning my back on God, living for myself, doing what my 'friends' told me to do, pursuing my destiny on my terms. I did not deserve God's welcome home. I did not expect his embrace, or his joy on my return. But there he was, ready and waiting to adopt me back into the family. You remind me of that arms-outstretched, joyful adoption moment. I hope you have felt it from me too.

This book is written for you. I could have filled

many more pages with all you have taught me about what it means to be an adopted child of God. I dearly hope that the words written here reflect to you not only the wonderful mystery of belonging to God's family, but something of my incredible love for you. I hope all my readers find delight and challenge and fresh insights and renewed grace and strength from grasping the miracle of their adoption, but I especially pray that you, with your backstage pass to the story behind the book, will recognise yourself on the pages, and see that you – just by being the wonderful you that you are – are making your indelible mark on the world.

Here's to the ongoing adoption adventure!
Your dad

Endnotes

Chapter One

1 See *The Lego Batman Movie*, Warner Bros., directed by Chris McKay, 2017.
2 Romans 8:1.
3 Romans 8:39.
4 Romans 8:28.
5 T.J. Burke, *Adopted into God's Family: Exploring Pauline Metaphor* (InterVarsity Press, 2006), p. 62. Octavian Augustus (27BC – AD14); Tiberius (AD14–37), Gaius Caligula (AD 37–41), Claudius (AD41–54) and Nero (AD54–68). '[A]doption was a means by which succession to power was brought about . . . successive Roman emperors adopted men not related to them by blood with the intention that the adoptee should succeed the emperor in the principate.'

Chapter Two

1 C. Hamilton, *Growth Fetish* (Allen & Unwin, 2003).

2 See J. Haidt, *The Coddling of the American Mind: How Good Intentions and Bad Ideas Are Setting Up a Generation for Failure* (Penguin, 2018).

3 Revelation 21:26 speaks about the glory of the nations being brought into the New Jerusalem, and the prophecy is full of references to every language being used to praise Christ.

4 See K. Kandiah, *God is Stranger* (Hodder & Stoughton, 2017).

5 F.F. Bruce, *Romans: An Introduction and Commentary*, vol. 6 (1985), p. 161. Biblical scholar F.F. Bruce explains that the word for condemnation is *katakrima*, and it carries the meaning of 'the punishment following sentence', or, in other words, penal servitude.

6 J.I. Packer, *Knowing God* (Hodder and Stoughton, 2005), pp. 206–7.

7 *The Princess Diaries*, (2001) Directed by Gary Marshall

8 Dietrich Bonhoeffer, *Letters and Papers from Prison* (Fontana, 1959), p. 173.

Chapter Three

1 Philip Melanchthon, 1531.

2 John 13:34–5.

3 Galatians 6:2.

4 Hebrews 10:25.

5 Hebrews 10:24.

6 John 19:26–8.

7 Matthew 15:3–4.

8 1 Timothy 5:1–2.

9 Romans 16:1,13.

Chapter Four

1 See M.D.S. Ainsworth & J. Bowlby, 'An Ethological Approach to Personality Development', *American Psychologist*, 46, 1991, pp. 331–41. https://fosteringandadoption.rip.org.uk/topics/ attachment-theory-research, accessed June 2019.

2 See http://www.mbird.com/2016/10/attach-ment-theory-and-your-relationship-with-god, accessed June 2019.

3 Matthew 6:5–6.

4 Romans 8:15.

5 Galatians 4:6.

6 J. Jeremias, 'The Key to Pauline Theology' (1964), p. 18, quoted in D. Bosch, *Witness to the World: The Christian Mission in Theological Perspective* (John Knox Press, 1980), p. 9.

7 See Matthew 6:7.

8 See Matthew 6:5.

Chapter Five

1 See C. Wright, *The Mission of God: Unlocking the Bible's Grand Narrative* (InterVarsity Press, 2007).

2 See K. Kandiah, *Destiny: What's Life All About?*

(Monarch, 2006); and also L. Newbigin, *Sin and Salvation* (SPCK, 1954).

3 Numbers 14:34 provides another perspective that the desert wandering was also punishment for their rebellion.

4 See A. Crouch, *Culture Making: Recovering Our Creative Calling* (InterVarsity Press, 2008).

5 Genesis 1:28.

6 Crouch, *Culture Making*, p. 23, citing cultural commentator Ken Myers.

7 For more information, visit www.homeforgood. org.uk

Chapter 6

1 M. Saunders (2017) 'There's a Single Christian Theme Running through Modern Cinema. Is God Speaking through Hollywood?' https:// www.christiantoday.com/article/theres-a-single-christian-theme-running-through-modern-cinema-is-god-speaking-through-holly-wood/104819.htm, accessed June 2019.

2 Genesis 1:26.

3 Psalm 110:1.

4 *Huiothesia* is the Greek term for adoption that Paul uses regularly in the New Testament. 'There are no biblical laws in the Old Testament governing the practice of huiothesia' (Burke, *Adopted into God's Family*, p. 47).

5 See Kandiah, *God is Stranger*, pp. 115–41.

6 See K. Kandiah, *Home for Good: Making a Difference for Vulnerable Children* (revised edition) (Hodder & Stoughton, 2019).

7 Eugene H. Peterson, *The Message: The Bible in Contemporary Language* (NavPress, 2002).

8 E. Peterson, *Eat This Book* (Hodder & Stoughton, 2006), p. 18.

9 Fifty per cent of male prisoners under 25 years old have experience of being in care (National Audit Office, 'Care Leavers' Transition to Adulthood', 2015, p. 5).

10 Luke 10, John 16.

11 Matthew 25.

Chapter 7

1 Luke 11:42, 46.

2 Luke 5:17–26.

3 Matthew 14:13–21.

4 Matthew 25:31–46.

5 James 1:27.

6 'The other NT references are in Acts 26:5, which employs it of Jewish worship and practice, and Col 2:18, where it is said to characterize a veneration devoted to or practiced by angels in the Colossian philosophy' (R.P. Martin, *Word Biblical Commentary*, Vol. 48 on James (Thomas Nelson, 1988), p. 52.

7 'Her priests do violence to my law and profane my holy things; they do not distinguish between the holy and the common; they teach that there is no difference between the unclean and the clean; and they shut their eyes to the keeping of my Sabbaths, so that I am profaned among them' (Ezekiel 22:26).

Chapter 8

1 Anne Longfield, the UK's Children's Commissioner, https://www.bbc.co.uk/news/education-44289645, accessed June 2019.

2 Sadly there are still those who make some unhelpful and dualistic assumptions about the gospel: see 'The Statement on Social Justice & the Gospel' by John MacArthur et al. https://statementonsocialjustice.com, accessed June 2019.

3 D. Bosch, *Witness to the World: The Christian Mission in Theological Perspective* (John Knox Press, 1980).

4 J.B. Payne, 'Justice'. In D.R.W. Wood, I.H. Marshall, A.R. Millard, J.I. Packer & D.J. Wiseman (Eds), *New Bible Dictionary* (3rd ed.) (InterVarsity Press, 1996), p. 634.

5 S.B. Ferguson & J.I. Packer, 'Justice'. In *New Dictionary of Theology* (electronic ed.) (InterVarsity Press, 2000), p. 359.

6 Quoted from HTB Leadership Conference 2018,

but see also B. Stevenson *Just Mercy: A Story of Justice and Redemption* (Scribe, 2015).
7 Matthew 6:33.

Chapter 9

1 D. Bonhoeffer, *The Cost of Discipleship* (SCM, 1996; German original 1937), p. 79.
2 Job 1–2 and 42.
3 Job 1:11.
4 Facebook post, 29/11/18 (used with permission).
5 F.I. Andersen, *Job: An Introduction and Commentary*, vol. 14 (InterVarsity Press, 1959), p. 262.
6 2 Timothy 3:12.
7 Job 31:16–23.
8 John 14:18.
9 T. Keller, 'The Christian's Happiness' https://www.monergism.com/christian's-happiness-romans-828-30.

Chapter 10

1 For more on this theme, see S. McKnight, *The Jesus Creed: Loving God, Loving Others* (Paraclete Press, 2009).
2 Romans 8: 22–4.
3 Revelation 7:9–10.
4 Exodus 20:8.
5 Luke 15:1–2.
6 Ephesians 2:13.

HODDER &
STOUGHTON

Hodder & Stoughton is the UK's
leading Christian publisher,
with a wide range of books from
the bestselling authors in the UK
and around the world ranging from
Christian lifestyle and theology to
apologetics, testimony and fiction.
We also publish the world's
most popular Bible translation
in modern English, the New
International Version, renowned
for its accuracy and readability.

Hodderfaith.com   Hodderbibles.co.uk
@HodderFaith   /HodderFaith